VOLUME II

Dining In — Baltimore

C O O K B O O K

A Collection of Gourmet Recipes for Complete Meals from the Baltimore Area's finest Restaurants

MARY LOU BAKER
BONNIE RAPOPORT MARSHALL

Foreword by
BROOKS ROBINSON

Peanut Butter Publishing
Seattle, Washington

HDL Publishing
Costa Mesa, California

Publisher: Elliott Wolf
Editor: Cherie Tucker
Coordinator: Bailey Alexander
Production: Melonie Branson
Illustration: Barbara Alexander
Imagesetting: Imageset Inc.

CONTENTS

TITLES IN SERIES

INTRODUCTION

Breezes refreshed with the salt of the Chesapeake Bay brush the faces of
visitors to Baltimore's Inner Harbor, and nose-tingling aromas of nutmeg
and cinnamon from the nearby McCormick Spice Company have for
years lent another sensual note to the downtown area. It is to the Inner
Harbor that tourists and residents gravitate, often overlooking the city's
neighborhoods where restaurants steeped in ethnic traditions would fill
an encyclopedia of nations.

Selecting twenty-one representatives of this restaurant-rich East Coast
city was a difficult task. What we have attempted to do is offer a cross-sec-
tion that reflects Baltimore's multi-faceted personality. It is a metropolis
that embraces the cuisines of many countries, and nurtures the traditions
of the people who migrated here in waves beginning in the 1700's and
continuing into the early part of the 20th century.

Little Italy, for instance, is home for more than two dozen fine eateries
within an eight block area. Each one of them would be considered a "find"
in itself, deserving attention by virtue of not only its food but its personal
management style by families who have passed the business from generation to generation. Oriental restaurants cater to Baltimoreans' fondness for
food from the Eastern hemisphere, ranging from authentic sushi at
Kawasaki and Shogun on Charles Street to Cantonese cuisine at Uncle
Lee's near the Memorial Stadium in northeast Baltimore.

A recent hotel boom has seen the opening of a half-dozen first-class hotel
restaurants catering to the discerning diner, and a rash of more casual
eateries has sprung up all over town to serve the growing number of
people who choose to live in such charming inner-city neighborhoods as
Federal Hill and Fells Point. Within the past several years, some 50 new
dining establishments have opened in Baltimore, bringing the total number of restaurants to well over two hundred.

The restaurants that appear in DINING IN BALTIMORE are all first-class,
most of them owner-operated (with the exception of the hotel properties),
and all of them staffed with chefs we consider to be exceptionally representative of their proud profession. As in any city, Baltimore natives are
often fickle when it comes to "favorites" and flock to the newest entry as
soon as its doors are open. Yet such venerable establishments as
Haussner's, Obrycki's and The Prime Rib have a loyal following of those
to whom "going out for dinner" means returning to their old haunts
where the maitres-d' know their names.

This book skims from the top, offering interviews and menus from twenty-one of Baltimore's finest restaurants that cooperated with us in preparing this book. Some of the recipes are simple enough for the novice while others require a certain skill. A few of the menus call for ingredients to be found in gourmet specialty shops, of which there are many in the Baltimore area. We suggest Morton's, the Gourmet Giant, the Gourmet Shop, Cross Street Market and Lexington Market as good local resources for ingredients. We have great respect for the professionals who contributed their time and talent to DINING IN BALTIMORE, and consider ourselves fortunate to live in a city where good eating is an everyday part of life. Maryland is a state abundantly blessed with the natural resources of the land and of the water, and with people who appreciate these finer things in life.

With whisk and chef's knife at the ready, read this book and enjoy!

Mary Lou Baker

Bonnie Rapoport Marshall

FOREWORD

"Welcome to Baltimore, a city I have come to love, a city on the move. Bonnie Rapoport Marshall, Mary Lou Baker and I invite you to join us in a sampling of Baltimore's finest restaurants. Dining in Baltimore is a culinary delight. Enjoy."

Bruce R. Johnson

DEDICATION:

To all of the talented chefs who gave so generously
of their time and knowledge - we thank you sincerely!

Bamboo House
RESTAURANT

Dinner for Four

Hot and Sour Soup

Shrimp with Snow Peas

Shrimp Toast

Orange Chicken

Shrimp in Lobster Sauce

Wine:

Wan-Fu
*(A French Bordeaux made especially
to compliment Oriental food)*

Owners: Joey and Connie Chiu

Chef: Joey Chiu

BAMBOO HOUSE

Food that I serve to the public must be as good as the food I serve to my own guests," says Joey Chiu, who with his wife, Connie, owns and operates the Bamboo House at Harborplace. Mr. Chiu is a talented chef, whose cooking at the original Bamboo House has captivated Baltimoreans since it opened.

Both restaurants have a particularly pleasant decor, with the Harborplace location enhanced by waterfront dining during warm weather. The interior color scheme is a study in soft shades of rose, with the plushly upholstered banquettes a favorite place among local professionals who meet here for lunch.

Connie Chiu serves as a charming hostess, recognizing regulars by both name and food preference. We, for instance, are known by our penchant for "Number 29," the numerical designation for the spicy orange chicken on the menu. Soft-shell crabs are an in-season specialty at the Harborplace Bamboo House, prepared with a black bean sauce, with aromatic spices, and with a Szechuan hot sauce that adds an exotic dimension to this Maryland delicacy.

Mr. Chiu, who plans the menus and trains his chefs, believes in blending fresh native ingredients with those indigenous to oriental cooking. "A plate of good cooking should not only look good, but taste good. It should also serve as a medium for introducing one's own culture to the public," says Mr. Chiu. Vegetables ranging from asparagus, broccoli, and snow peas to bok choy and bamboo shoots are used for color and texture. Fresh fish is very much a part of the daily specials. Monkfish, grouper, and sole are offered along with shrimp, scallops, chicken, pork, and lamb preparations that comprise the regular menu.

Consistent is a word to describe the fare at Bamboo House. Because of Mr. Chiu's careful management and his skillful kitchen staff, one may take guests here confidently time after time. What Mr. and Mrs. Chiu call "guest relations" is translated into good service and a welcoming atmosphere, both essential ingredients for a successful restaurant. Bamboo House serves Hunan/Szechuan, Cantonese, and Shanghai-style cuisine with style and a smile.

Pratt Street Pavilion
Harborplace, Baltimore, Maryland
(301) 625-1191

HOT AND SOUR SOUP

3 cups of chicken broth
   Salt and pepper, to taste

1/2 cup shredded lean pork
   (first slice, then cut each
   slice into thin strips)

1/2 cup tiger lily buds, soaked in
   lukewarm water for 20
   minutes, drained and cut
   into 1" pieces

4 fresh mushrooms, cleaned and
   diced, or 4 dried black
   Chinese mushrooms,
   soaked in lukewarm water
   for 20 minutes, drained and
   diced.

1 to 2 squares bean curd (tofu),
   chopped

2 tablespoons chopped green
   onion (white part only)

1/4 cup of soy sauce

3 tablespoons of vinegar

1 tablespoon of cornstarch
   dissolved in 2 tablespoons
   of water

2 eggs, beaten
   A few drops of sesame oil

1/4 teaspoon MSG

1. Put the chicken broth in a saucepan and bring it to a boil.

2. Add remaining ingredients to the chicken broth except the cornstarch, eggs, sesame oil and MSG. Bring to a boil again, lower the heat and simmer for 2 to 3 minutes.

3. Stir in the cornstarch mixture. Once it thickens the soup, blend in the beaten eggs, stirring well. The eggs should cook into large curds.

4. Add a few drops of sesame oil and the MSG. Serve.

Note: Tiger lily buds, also known as golden needles, once soaked, must have their knobby ends cut off. They are good in stir-fries since they absorb and lend flavor. Bean curd, also known as tofu, is made of soybean powder and comes in square cakes that measure about 3" per side. They are white and spongy. If submerged in water that is replenished every few days, they will stay fresh for up to 5 days. Bean curd is bland but absorbent, and adaptable to all types of cooking - simmering, steaming, stir-frying. It is highly nutritious.

SHRIMP WITH SNOW PEAS

1 pound large shrimp, cleaned, shelled and deveined

1 egg white
Pepper, to taste

3 cups peanut or Wesson oil

1/2 pound snow peas, washed and strings removed

1 tablespoon chopped green onion (white part only)

Salt and sugar, to taste

Pinch of MSG

3/4 to 1 cup of chicken broth

2 teaspoons cornstarch dissolved in 2 tablespoons of chicken broth

1. Marinate the shrimp with the egg white and pepper for 30 minutes.
2. Heat a wok hot and dry. Add the oil. When it is beginning to smoke, add the shrimp and snow peas, stirring for 1 minute. Drain, reserving 2 to 3 tablespoons of oil.
3. Return the reserved oil to the wok. Stir-fry the chopped onion for 1/2 minute.
4. Return the shrimp and snow peas to the wok. Add salt, sugar, MSG, 3/4 cup chicken broth and cornstarch mixture. Let everything come to a boil and thicken. Add additional broth if too thick.
5. Toss the contents of the wok so they are coated with sauce. Transfer to a platter and serve.

Snow peas are used mainly in Cantonese dishes to give a crunchy texture and bright green color. They should be rinsed and have the strings along their sides removed. They will keep fresh, sealed in a plastic bag and refrigerated for 5 to 6 days. Although frozen pea pods may be substituted, the texture of the fresh peas cannot be surpassed!

Note: It is important never to add oil to a wok until it is hot. This prevents sticking.

SHRIMP TOAST

1/4 pounds small shrimp (peeled)	1 teaspoon flour
6 whole waterchestnuts	1 egg (white only)
1/4 teaspoon salt	3 teaspoons of oil
1/4 teaspoon of garlic powder	2 pieces of bread
1/4 teaspoon of baking powder	

1. Wash and dry the shrimp.
2. Grind shrimp and waterchestnuts in a food processor.
3. Add salt, garlic powder, baking powder, flour and egg white to the ground paste; mix thoroughly.
4. Add 3 teaspoons of cooking oil to the paste and mix again.
5. Spread the paste onto two pieces of bread; deep fry until golden brown; cut into quarters and serve.

ORANGE FLAVORED CHICKEN

CHICKEN

3 boneless chicken legs, skinned	1 tablespoon cornstarch
1 egg, beaten	2 tablespoons oil
1 tablespoon flour	

1. Dice the chicken meat.
2. Mix together egg, 1 tablespoon flour, 1 tablespoon cornstarch, and toss chicken in mixture. Then add 2 tablespoons of oil to mixture and toss again. (Oil will keep the chicken pieces from sticking together.)
3. Deep-fry the chicken meat in hot oil until golden brown.
4. Drain on paper towel and set aside.
5. In saucepan, heat ORANGE SAUCE until boiling, then put in the fried chicken pieces. Mix evenly and serve with rice.

ORANGE SAUCE
(Prepare a day ahead)

6 tablespoons sugar

10 tablespoons of soy sauce

1 rind of a whole orange, cut
  into small pieces

3 tablespoons of cooking wine

3 tablespoons of water

1. Stir together all the sauce ingredients until the sugar dissolves.
2. Leave mixture in refrigerator overnight.

SHRIMP IN LOBSTER SAUCE

4 cups of chicken broth

2 tablespoons of ground pork

1 pound of shrimp (size 16-20),
  peeled and cleaned

1/2 teaspoon of salt

1/4 teaspoon of pepper

3 tablespoons of cornstarch

1/3 cup water

2 eggs, beaten

1 stalk spring onion - chopped

1. Pour 4 cups of chicken broth into a pot; add the ground pork, salt, and pepper; heat until boiling.
2. Put shrimp into the pot and cook until pink (3-4 minutes).
3. Mix 3 tablespoons of cornstarch with 1/3 cup of water; pour the cornstarch into the pot while stirring.
4. Stir in beaten eggs.
5. Transfer the mixture onto a serving plate, sprinkle chopped onion on top and serve with rice.

   Note: In Chinese cooking, the designation "lobster sauce" is not literal.

THE
BRASS ELEPHANT

Dinner for Four

Baked Clams Santa Lucia

Lasagna Di Carnivale

Cioppino Alla Brass Elephant

Broccoli San Vincente

Strawberry Tart with Chocolate and Spun Sugar

Wines:

Laurent Perrier Ultra Brut, N.V.
Gattinara, Dr. Marion Antoniolo, 1979
Gavi, Bersano, 1983 or Fume Blanc, Robert Mondavi, 1985

Owners: Country Fare Group

Chef: Randy Stahl

BRASS ELEPHANT

Loving, hands-on attention to both food and service explain the success of the Brass Elephant, one of four Baltimore area restaurants owned and operated by a group that is involved as chefs, maitre-d's, and managers of their dining establishments. Chef Randy Stahl and manager Jack Elsby have been involved with the Brass Elephant since it opened. "The harder we work, the luckier we get," says Elsby, who is known in the local community as a person who contributes his energies to worthy civic causes.

Situated in a restored townhouse built in 1851, the premises of the Brass Elephant are distinguished by the elegance of a bygone era, while the food is thoroughly au courant. Northern Italian is the accent of the kitchen, where chef Stahl and his staff specialize in homemade pasta, rich sauces, and such classics as saltimbocca, shrimp scampi, and sweetbreads prepared with a sauce of Marsala wine and cream.

Born in Brooklyn and trained at the Culinary Institute of America, Stahl was a chef at Sal Anthony's in Manhattan before coming to Baltimore in 1980 to cook at Fiori's, another of the Country Fare Group's restaurants. With a bachelor's degree in business from the University of Pittsburgh, he blends his creative talents with a cool head for pleasing customers who expect and receive good value for their dollar at his tables.

Stahl's repertoire is not limited to northern Italian cuisine. Grilled tuna or swordfish with lime butter and macadamia or pine nuts are among his specialties, as are scallops with an almond sauté. "Being in Baltimore makes me more seafood-conscious," says Stahl, who likes to shop for his own supplies at local city markets.

Diners who enjoy the results of his labor do so in rooms decorated with teak panelling fashioned by Moroccan craftsmen hired by the building's second owner, a clipper ship captain whose legacy also includes a Tiffany glass skylight dome, chandeliers of Waterford and of Czechoslovakian crystal, and brass wall sconces from a Bavarian castle.

"Where ever is my love, there is my heart" reads the inscription over the fireplace, and at the Brass Elephant it is obvious that the hearts of the owners are on North Charles Street.

924 North Charles Street
Baltimore, Maryland
(301) 547-8480

BAKED CLAMS SANTA LUCIA

24 *little neck clams*
24 *sliced cooked mushrooms*
1/4 *pound of backfin crabmeat*
   tossed with 1 teaspoon of
   finely diced prosciutto ham

1/2 *pound SEASONED BUTTER*
   for topping clams

1. Shuck clams, top with crabmeat, slice of mushroom and a teaspoon of seasoned butter.
2. Place clams on a bed of rock salt to level clam so butter will not run out when hot. Bake at 450° for 10-12 minutes or until heated through and browned.

SEASONED BUTTER

3 *cloves of garlic*
1 *large shallot*
2 *anchovy filets*
1 *pimento filet*
1/2 *pound sweet butter, softened*

Pinch of Romano cheese
1 *tablespoon parsley, chopped*
1 *ounce white wine*
Black pepper, to taste

1. Chop first four ingredients in food processor until fine.
2. Add softened butter, Romano, parsley, white wine, pepper and blend until incorporated.

LASAGNA DI CARNIVALE

LASAGNA NOODLES
  (recipe follows)
1-1/2 pounds ricotta cheese
   3 ounces grated Romano cheese
   2 whole eggs
   5 ounces cooked, chopped spinach
     Salt and black pepper, to taste
 1/2 pound sliced mozzarella

1 tablespoon each fresh oregano
   and basil
   (or 1/2 teaspoon each dried)
2 tablespoons chopped parsley
1-1/2 pints meat sauce
   5 ounces sliced cooked mushrooms
 1/2 pound sliced cooked sausage

1. Combine ricotta and Romano cheeses, eggs, and spinach; season with salt, black pepper, oregano, basil and chopped parsley.

2. Place layer of noodles in baking pan; spoon approximately 4 ounces cold meat sauce over noodles.

3. Dot cheese mixture over meat sauce; layer with mushrooms, sausage, and sliced mozzarella cheese.

4. Start another layer of noodles and repeat layers twice again, finishing with noodles and meat sauce.

5. Cover with foil and bake 40 minutes at 350° or until the lasagna is slightly puffed.

6. Let cool 20-30 minutes and serve with remaining meat sauce.

NOODLE DOUGH

10 ounces durum wheat flour
 5 ounces semolina
 1 teaspoon olive oil

Pinch of salt
Approximately 2 tablespoons
   of cold water
2 whole eggs

1. Combine all ingredients except water.

2. Knead until smooth, adding water as necessary.

3. Roll through pasta machine until thickness of a dime. Cut into 2" wide strips.

4. Cook in salted, boiling water until al dente. (3-4 minutes) Drain.

5. Shock the noodles in cold water and hold until ready to use.

CIOPPINO ALLA BRASS ELEPHANT

1 clove garlic, cracked

1/4 cup olive oil

16 little neck clams

24 cultured mussels

1 pound squid cleaned,
   sliced and cooked

1 pound sea scallops

1 pound king crab legs, split

16 jumbo shrimp

4 ounces dry white wine

2 ounces dry vermouth

1 pound linguini, cooked

1. Brown cracked garlic in olive oil, then add seafood and cover.
2. Braise the seafood for 5 minutes and add 4 ounces of dry white wine and 2 ounces of dry vermouth.
3. Add 2 cups of the following SAUCE and steam until the seafood is just done.
4. Serve over linguine cooked al dente.

SAUCE FOR CIOPPINO

2 ounces olive oil

1/2 onion sliced thin

2 leeks sliced thin and washed
   several times in cold water

1/8 head of red cabbage sliced thin
   (blanch in boiling salted
   water and cool; add at the
   end)

6 cloves garlic, finely chopped

1 can Italian peeled plum
   tomatoes (35 ounce size)

1 cup of dry white wine

1 bay leaf

1/4 teaspoon thyme

1/2 teaspoon oregano

1 tablespoon basil

Salt and pepper, to taste

1. Sauté onions, leeks and garlic in olive oil.
2. Add spices and white wine, boil to reduce by half. Add the tomatoes, (roughly chopped).
3. Simmer mixture for 30 minutes and add cabbage. Adjust seasonings to taste.

BROCCOLI SAN VINCENTE

2 *pounds trimmed broccoli,*
 blanched in boiling salted
 water.

TOPPING FOR BROCCOLI

8 *ounces sour cream*
2 *ounces grated Swiss cheese*
 Pinch of Romano cheese
 Salt and black pepper to taste

Juice of 1 lemon
Zest of 1 lemon, blanched 30
 seconds in boiling water
Toasted sliced almonds

1. Combine the ingredients for the topping.
2. Spoon over hot broccoli and place under broiler until hot. Garnish with toasted sliced almonds

STRAWBERRY TART FILLED WITH CHOCOLATE AND COVERED WITH SPUN SUGAR

1 quart fresh strawberries

TART DOUGH

2-1/2 *cups of flour*
1/3 *cup of sugar*
1/4 *cup of sweet butter*

1 *beaten egg*
Ice water

1. Sift together flour and sugar.
2. Cut in butter until bits of butter are the size of rice.
3. Add egg and enough water to bring dough into a ball - refrigerate for one hour.
4. Roll out to 1/8" thickness and line a 10" tart pan. Let rest for 1/2 hour.
5. Fill with pie weights and bake at 400° for 12 minutes. Remove pie weights, reduce heat to 375° and bake till golden brown, about 12 minutes. Cool.

PASTRY CREAM

1 *pint milk, scalded*
4 *ounces of sugar*
2 *ounces of cornstarch*
1 *teaspoon gelatin*
1/2 *cup of milk*

3 *eggs*
2 *ounces sweet butter*
Dash of vanilla
2 *ounces of melted sweet chocolate*

1. Sift together sugar, cornstarch, and gelatin.
2. Add 1/2 cup cold milk, eggs, and scalded milk, mix well and cook over double boiler until thick.
3. Remove from heat and add chocolate, butter, and vanilla; refrigerate until cold.
4. When chilled, fill tart shell with pastry cream. Cover cream with fresh strawberries.

BRASS ELEPHANT

SPUN SUGAR

Right before serving make spun sugar.

1 cup sugar

1. Heat sugar in medium saucepan stirring continuously until melted and amber in color.
2. Remove from heat and cool until thin strands of sugar form from the end of a spoon when it is waved back and forth.
3. Over the finished tart, wave a spoon back and forth constantly dipping it back into the sugar until top of tart is covered with thin webs of sugar.
4. Serve immediately.

CAFE DES ARTISTES

Dinner for Eight

Bisque De Homard

Ravioli à La Grecque

Salad Provençale

Medallions Du Boeuf Au Poivre

Legumes Hollandaise

Gateau à L'École

Wines:

*Spottswood Sauvignon Blanc, Chateau Oliver Graves,
Sterling Diamond Mountain Ranch Cabernet Sauvignon,
William Hill Gold Label Chardonnay 1985*

Owners: Ann and Harvey Clapp

Chef: Gerard Boisman

CAFE DES ARTISTES

Music, art, and magic are components of the alchemy at Cafe des Artistes, a sophisticated dining establishment favored by its neighbors in north Baltimore as well as discerning diners citywide. Light jazz and semi-classical favorites are live on the baby grand, paintings from a nearby art gallery grace the walls, and an amateur magician (who doubles as a bartender) entertains patrons in the well-appointed lounge.

Owners Ann and Harvey Clapp have a success story on their hands. Much of the credit must go to the Cafe's 33-year-old chef, Gerard Boisman, a graduate of L'Ecole Hotelier in Paris. Boisman's intelligence and quick sense of humor overflow into his culinary philosophy, yeilding one of the most eclectic menus in the book. He combines the natural flavors of food with an artistic eye that inspires such visual whimsies as pheasant with stripes of red, white, and blue sauces in honor of the Fourth of July.

Seasonal specialties are featured on an auxiliary menu that changes nightly at Cafe des Artistes. In mid-July, for instance, one would find fresh softshell crabs coated with crushed sesame seeds, velvety avocado soup seasoned with fresh dill cut from the chef's window garden, ripe melon and Maryland tomatoes combined in a Salad Provençal, and a cognac-kissed Maine lobster bisque.

Boisman balances his regular customers' tastes with healthful eating habits. He has taken an imaginative step in catering to the American taste for red meat by serving medallions of beef in a choice of small, medium, and large portions. He also has created several low-calorie dishes, among them chicken breast poached with leeks in white wine, and flounder filets wrapped in lettuce poached in white wine. Maitre-d' Billy Mettawiparee works with Mr. Clapp in selecting the stunning collection of 132 wines.

Cafe des Artistes is well-endowed with graceful service, good food, and a tastefully executed atmosphere that reflects the personal predilections of the Clapps. One comes here to be elegantly entertained and is rarely disappointed.

1501 Sulgrave Avenue
Baltimore, Maryland
(301) 664-2200

BISQUE DE HOMARD
Lobster Bisque

BASE

2 *small live lobsters, steamed*	2 *whole cloves*
1 *carrot*	1 *teaspoon Italian seasoning*
1 *medium onion*	2 *teaspoons salt*
2 *tomatoes*	1 *teaspoon black pepper*
1 *branch celery*	1/2 *gallon water*
4 *cloves garlic*	

BISQUE

1 *quart whipping cream*	1 *pinch whole saffron*
2 *fluid ounces of Cognac (or brandy)*	1/2 *teaspoon paprika*
2 *teaspoons flour*	*Cayenne pepper and*
1 *teaspoon butter*	*salt, to taste*
2 *teaspoons tomato paste*	

1. Separate the tail from the body of the lobsters by twisting and pulling at the same time. Peel the shell off the tail and keep the meat and large segments of the claws refrigerated.

2. Chop the tail shell, body, first two segments of the claws and all the washed vegetables into 1" cube chunks, using a cleaver or large French knife.

3. In a stock pot, cover all the ingredients of the base with the cold water and bring slowly to a simmering point. Skim as often as needed and let simmer for about 45 minutes.

4. Meanwhile, crack the large segments of the claws and extract the meat, trying not to break it. Split the meat lengthwise and sauté it in 2 tablespoons of butter on very low heat for a few seconds. Devein the tails and dice them into 1/4" to 1/2" cubes.

5. Put no more than a cup at a time of the base ingredients, half solids, half liquid in the food processor. Turn on, holding the appliance firmly and let run until smooth. Empty into a very fine sieve and repeat operation until exhaustion of all ingredients. Press the base through the sieve with a ladle, emptying the dry shell particles often.

6. Heat 1 quart of the base, adding in the tomato paste and spices. When boiling, skim, add the cream and the Cognac. Bring to simmering again, skimming as often as needed.

7. Separately, melt the butter, stir in the flour and cook slowly, mixing constantly.

8. Whisk in the roux by small quantities until desired consistency is reached. Check and adjust the seasoning. A few minutes before serving, add the diced meat.

9. When serving with a ladle, make sure to include some of the meat with each serving. Lay half a sautéed claw over each serving. At the right consistency, the bisque should barely support the half claws at its surface.

Note: The excess base without any cream, if any, may be poured into an ice cube tray and frozen. The lobster-base cubes can be kept together in a plastic bag in the freezer and used later as the base for bisque, Newburg sauce, etc.

RAVIOLI à LA GRECQUE
Greek Style Ravioli

8 ounces ground lamb meat
8 ounces feta cheese
4 teaspoons fresh chopped basil
2 cloves garlic
1 lemon
   Salt, pepper to taste
4 8" X 12" fresh egg pasta sheets
1 egg

2 teaspoons olive oil
   Flour
   Warm water
1 gallon boiling water
1/2 cup oil
3-4 tablespoons butter
2 ounces Ouzo or other anise-flavored brandy

1. Season and sauté ground lamb in olive oil over medium heat. When cooked and still hot, mix in the chopped garlic. Let cool.

2. In mixer bowl put together the crumbled feta cheese, cold lamb meat, chopped basil and juice of the lemon.

3. To prepare pasta: Sprinkle flour on a flat, clean and dry surface. Lay a clean, dry towel on a table. If the pasta sheets do not stick to the finger when pressed, dampen no more than two sheets at a time in a shallow pan filled with warm water. Carefully lift the sheets of pasta out of the water. Sponge the water off with the towel and lay on the floured surface.

4. Brush the beaten egg over whole sheet. Space 12 spoonfuls of meat filling - 3 in the width and 4 in the length - over the sheet no closer than 1/2" from the edges. Cover with other sheet slightly and carefully stretched.

5. Run a ravioli cutting wheel between the little mounds of stuffing and around the edges of the sheet. Pick up the formed ravioli, place on cookie sheet, and refrigerate. Proceed with second set of sheets.

6. Meanwhile bring one gallon of salted water and oil to a light boil. Carefully immerse the ravioli in the water, leave them in for about four minutes, lift them out, lay them flat on a buttered dish and keep until serving time.

7. At serving time, melt the butter in skillet, slide in the ravioli and sauté on low heat. Off the stove, sprinkle with ouzo and ignite. Lay 3 ravioli per plate and sprinkle with freshly chopped parsley.

SALADE PROVENÇALE
Provençale Salad

1 head romaine lettuce	*4 ripe tomatoes*
8 ounces fresh goat cheese	*1 small cantaloupe*

DRESSING

2 large garlic cloves, minced	*1/2 cup lemon juice*
1 cup olive oil	

1. Put the ingredients of the dressing in a blender at high speed for about three minutes or until very smooth. Empty through a very fine strainer and keep refrigerated.

2. Wash and cut the romaine into large pieces. Cut the cantaloupe into 1" slices, peel them and cut them into diamond-shaped pieces. Cut the top and the bottom off the tomatoes and into two thick slices. Cut the fresh goat cheese into 8-1 ounce slices.

3. On chilled plates, lay a bed of lettuce, a slice of tomato over the center, pieces of cantaloupe around and a slice of cheese atop the tomato. Mix dressing ingredients, and sprinkle over each salad before serving.

MEDALLIONS DU BOEUF AU POIVRE
Beef tenderloin slices in pepper sauce

6 to 8 pounds beef tenderloin
6 ounces cracked black pepper
Salt to taste
2 ounces butter

8 fluid ounces Cognac
(or brandy)
1 pint whipping cream
1/2 teaspoon demiglace
(or beef base)

1. Cut about 1-1/2" of the tips off a well-trimmed whole tenderloin and cut into 32 slices of equal thickness.

2. Lay out the medallions and sprinkle them with cracked black pepper to taste. Rub the pepper into the meat and repeat operation on other side. Cover with waxed paper or film and let sit in refrigerator for a few hours. The coating with pepper should be moderate, especially with freshly cracked pepper, in order not to overpower the flavor of the meat.

3. At serving time, salt the medallions to taste, heat the butter in a skillet, and gently lay the medallions in the very hot but not burning butter. Cook no more than two minutes on each side for medium rare.

4. Remove from burner and pour the Cognac over the medallions. Return to stove and ignite the Cognac. Before the flame burns out, pour the cream over the meat.

5. Remove the meat to a platter and cover with an inverted plate. Turn the heat on maximum under the sauce to obtain a strong boiling.

6. At that point the meat should be undercooked. Even though off the burner, it will continue cooking with residual heat.

7. Let the sauce reduce until it reaches the consistency of a light custard. If the cream reduces too much and breaks, quickly add one fluid ounce of milk and cook down again until right consistency. Optionally, add in a half teaspoon of beef demiglace, turn off the heat and let cool.

8. Lay four medallions on each plate, slightly overlapping each other.

9. Spoon the sauce over the meat. At the right consistency, the sauce should be smooth and remain on the meat, barely running down.

10. Serve immediatel;y.

Note: To clean tenderloin, remove all tendons and fat. You will lose approximately 1 1/2 pounds of the original weight.

LEGUMES HOLLANDAISE

Steam separately until tender:

2 *cups broccoli flowerets*	2 *cups cauliflowerets*

HOLLANDAISE GERARD

1 *pound butter (unsalted)*	1 *tablespoon lemon juice.*
2 *egg yolks*	*Salt and cayenne pepper, to taste*
2 *ice cubes*	

1. Melt butter slowly, skimming solids from top

2. Heat drawn butter until color lightens.

3. In food processor, place 2 egg yolks and ice cubes. On high speed, whip until ice is crushed and melted. Turn motor off, scrape sides quickly, and reactivate on high speed while slowly adding hot butter until mixture is thickened.

4. Add lemon juice, salt, and cayenne pepper to taste.

5. Nap steamed vegetables with hollandaise and serve as side-dish.

Note: If hollandaise is too thick, add 1 tablespoon of warm water to obtain desired consistency. If during the blender process, the hollandaise separates, add 1 tablespoon cold water and re-start motor.

CAFE DES ARTISTES

GATEAU À L'ÉCOLE

Created by Jan Bandula of the Baltimore Culinary Art Institute and adapted for home execution.

CHOCOLATE CAKE

1 9" *chocolate cake prepared according to your favorite recipe.*

MERINGUE

4 *egg whites*
4 *ounces granulated sugar*

1/2 *teaspoon vanilla extract*

1. In mixer, whip the egg whites and add half of the sugar before they are completely stiff.
2. When stiff, fold in the rest of the sugar and the vanilla extract.
3. On a sheet of waxed paper, draw a 9 1/2" circle.
4. Spread the meringue with a spatula over the whole circle or pipe with a pastry bag in spirals from the circumference to the center.
5. Bake at 225° to 250° for at least 2 hours.

BUTTER CREAM

2 1/2 *ounces of sugar*
2 *tablespoons of water*
2 *egg yolks*

2 1/2 *ounces of butter*
1 *teaspoon coffee extract*

1. Boil the sugar with 2 tablespoons of water until slightly thick.
2. Pour over the egg yolks in a small bowl and beat rapidly.
3. Beat until cool; add the soft (but not melted) butter and the coffee extract.

GANACHE

8 ounces semi-sweet chocolate   *1 cup whipping cream*

1. Boil the cream for a few minutes.
2. Melt the chocolate in a double boiler or for no more than 45 seconds in the microwave oven.
3. Mix with the boiled cream.
4. Let cool to room temperature.

FINAL PREPARATION

1. Peel the upper and lower crusts off the cake and cut into two equal slices. Optionally, brush a mixture of equal parts of water and rum onto both slices.
2. Spread equal amounts of butter cream on each slice of cake. Lay the meringue over one of the slices and reverse the other slice over the meringue.
3. Press slightly together and with a serrated knife, trim the different layers to a uniform wall. Make sure to trim the crust off of the chocolate cake. Lay the cake on a cardboard circle.
4. Put the cake on a clean, smooth counter or table and pour the still liquid ganache all over the cake. Make sure to start close to the edges allowing the ganache to run down the sides evenly. Finish with a small amount in the center. The ganache, if at the right consistency, should coat the entire cake without the use of a spatula but should not completely run off the side.
5. If a spatula is needed to spread the too-thick ganache or to pick the too-thin ganache off of the table, pour it back on the cake. Avoid pressure on the layers which will create crumbs that will eventually appear in the smooth coating of the ganache.
6. Refrigerate immediately.

Chez Fernand

Dinner for Four

Gravlax

Asparagus with Two Sauces

Bouillabaisse

Pear Soufflé with Chocolate Sauce

Wines:

with Bouillabaise: Hermitage White (Cote Du Rhone)
with Pear Soufflé: Sauternes

Owners/Operators: Fernand and Odette Tergisguel

Chef: Michel Tergisguel

CHEZ FERNAND

We will be the best or nothing," is the philosophy of Fernand Tergisguel, the energetic and likeable owner-operator of Chez Fernand next to Baltimore's historic Shot Tower. A native of Quempir, Fernand was trained in France and came with his wife, Odette, to New York in 1963. There he worked under Rene Verdon, became well-known as the chef at Du Midi, and eventually opened his own restaurant.

During a visit to Maryland in 1972, he decided to abandon Manhattan in favor of a more self-fulfilling lifestyle in "the land of pleasant living." When a fire destroyed the first Chez Fernand in 1984, Fernand and his wife opened a larger establishment in downtown Baltimore, which immediately won favor among those who appreciate good food, good wine, and good fellowship.

Fernand runs his restaurant with a sure hand, greeting many of the clients by name and keeping a close eye on the kitchen. It is here that his son, a recent graduate of the Culinary Institute of America in Hyde Park, presides. "It is when I burn myself at the stove that I realize I am not a machine," says the 23-year-old Michel. Assisted by longtime Chez Fernand sous-chef, Gary Cramblitt, Michel produces food that is fresh, flavorful, and true to his country-French origins.

He and his father shop together for the freshest local produce, to keep them stocked with morels from Oregon, halibut from France, sole from England, raspberries from New Zealand, and salmon from Scandinavia.

One of the more tragic aspects of the fire that destroyed the original Chez Fernand was the loss of the priceless wine cellar. Aided by a network of French vineyards, M. Tergisguel has been able to rebuild his wine list to an exceptional level of excellence and variety.

One of the best annual parties in Baltimore is the invitation-only November celebration of the arrival of the nouveau beaujolais from France. Chez Fernand's rustic upper rooms are popular year-round for private dinner parties and business meetings. Chez Fernand has earned a special place in Baltimore, demonstrating that persistence in the face of great odds pays off.

805 East Fayette Street
Baltimore, Maryland
(301) 752-8030

GRAVLAX

5-1/2 ounces sugar
2-1/2 ounces salt
   3 teaspoons white peppercorns
   3 tablespoons juniper berries
   1 bunch of fresh dill
   5 red onions, sliced
   4 lemons, sliced
 16 lemons, juiced
   1 side of salmon filet, scaled

Mix first four ingredients. Layer long roasting or ceramic container pan with half of sliced lemons, onions, and dill. Place the salmon on top. Cover with lemon juice and marinade; marinate covered in refrigerator for 3-5 days. Slice thinly on the bias and serve with SAUCE.

SAUCE FOR GRAVLAX

1/4 cup of the gravlax marinade
1/2 cup vegetable oil
  4 egg yolks
  2 tablespoons mustard (optional)
1/4 cup fresh chopped dill

Place yolks and marinade in a bowl with mustard. Whip and add oil little by little until emulsified. Add fresh chopped dill.

ASPARAGUS WITH TWO SAUCES

16 *peeled trimmed asparagus*   *Boiling water, salted*

When water is boiling, add asparagus. Cook until bright green and tender. Shock in ice cold water to preserve color. Served wrapped with HOLLANDAISE MICHEL or drizzled with VINAIGRETTE.

HOLLANDAISE MICHEL

2 *egg yolks*   *White wine*
   Cayenne pepper (pinch)   *Lemon juice*
   Salt and pepper   1 *pound clarified butter*

Whip eggs, seasoning, and white wine with wire whisk in double boiler. Add the butter and continue whipping until thickened.

VINAIGRETTE

1/3 *cup vinegar*   *Herbs Provençe*
1/3 *cup oil*   1 *teaspoon French mustard*
     Salt and pepper

Note: Herbs Provençe are a blend of tarragon, thyme, lavender, dill, etc., sold in gourmet shops. They add a wonderful flavor to soups, sauces, and salad dressings.

BOUILLABAISSE

8 tablespoons olive oil	8 medium shrimp, shelled
1 leek, julienne	1/2 pound sea scallops
1/2 onion, sliced	2 small lobsters, shelled

2 cloves garlic, chopped
  large pinch saffron
  pinch fennel seed
	1 dozen mussels,
	  cleaned and debearded
	  FISH STOCK (recipe follows)

2 tomatoes, peeled and chopped	Splash of white wine

1 pound grouper filets,
  cut into pieces
	Cayenne pepper, salt and
	  cracked black pepper, to taste

1 pound perch filets,
  cut into pieces
	Chopped parsley
	HOMEMADE CROUTONS
	  (recipe follows)

1 pound monkfish filets, cut into pieces	

1. Heat olive oil in a very large pot.
2. Add onion, leeks, garlic, saffron. Sauté for 1 minute.
3. Add fennel, tomatoes and all seafood. Sauté for a couple of seconds.
4. Add FISH STOCK with a touch of white wine, salt and peppers to taste.
5. Bring to boil. Simmer, covered, (4-5 minutes).
6. Adjust seasonings. Remove to serving dish.
7. Garnish with croutons and chopped parsley. Serve with bowls of grated cheese, ROUILLE and AIOLI on the side.

Note: You may substitute any white, firm-fleshed fish that is available. Also, add tarragon or basil according to individual preferences.

CROUTONS

1 loaf of day old French bread
1 cup olive oil

1 tablespoon paprika

1. Heat olive oil and paprika in large frying pan.
2. Cut bread into cubes.
3. Toss cubes in hot oil and sauté until browned.
4. Drain on paper towels and store in covered container until ready to use.

ROUILLE

3 each red peppers and pimentos
4 egg yolks
  Cayenne

2 tablespoons garlic, chopped
  Salt and pepper, to taste
8 ounces olive oil

1. Purée pimentos and red peppers.
2. Add yolks, cayenne pepper, garlic and salt and pepper to taste.
3. Whip and slowly incorporate olive oil until consistency of thick vinaigrette (mayonnaise). Correct seasoning.

AIOLI

1/2 cup potatoes, peeled and
　　chunked
　　FISH STOCK, enough to cover
　　potatoes
　　Cayenne pepper

4 egg yolks
4 tablespoons garlic, chopped
　Chopped parsley to garnish

1. Cook potatoes in fish stock until well done. Purée.
2. Add cayenne pepper, egg yolk and chopped garlic.
3. Incorporate olive oil until very thick mayonnaise-like consistency.
4. Correct seasonings. Garnish with chopped parsley.

*Note: Serve ROUILLE and AIOLI in bowls as garnish for BOUIL-
LABAISSE. Accompany with loaves of French bread to absorb the soup
juices.*

FISH STOCK

2 tablespoons butter
　Mirepoix:
　3 leeks, white part only
　2 ribs celery, diced medium
　2 onions, diced medium
　1 tablespoon garlic, minced
2 tomatoes, chopped
5 pounds flatfish bones

1/4 cup white wine
　Basil, to taste
　Bay leaf
　White pepper
　Parsley stems
　Thyme, to taste
　Salt, to taste

1. Melt butter in a flat-bottomed pan. Sauté mirepoix until vegetables are
   tender. Add bones, sauté 1 minute. Add tomatoes.
2. Deglaze with white wine, stirring constantly.
3. Add water to cover and bring to a boil. Simmer. Skim scum from top
   of stock without stirring.
4. Add herbs. Cook 45 minutes. Strain.

PEAR SOUFFLÉ WITH CHOCOLATE SAUCE

Base:

6-1/2 ounces milk
3 egg yolks
1-2 teaspoons vanilla

2 tablespoons Chambord or
  Grand Marnier
1/4 ounces cornstarch
1 ounce sugar

1. Mix all ingredients except milk and liqueur in bowl. Bring milk to a boil and add half of it to previous mixture. After that is well blended, add to remaining milk and mix well.
2. Bring mixture to a boil, whipping vigorously. Set aside. Add Chambord or Grand Marnier if desired.
3. Whisk in PEAR PURÉE (recipe follows)

PEAR PURÉE

8 pears (peeled, cored)
2 cups SIMPLE SYRUP (See Index
  for recipe.)

1/8 teaspoon cinnamon
  Juice of one orange
  Juice of one lemon

Cook all ingredients in simple syrup until the pears are very soft. Purées in blender.

Assembly: Butter 4 small soufflé molds and dust with sugar. Soften BASE in bowl. For each soufflé, beat 3 egg whites until they form soft peaks, then add 1/2 ounce of sugar. Fold egg white mixture into softened BASE. Pour into molds and bake at 350° for approximately 16 minutes. Serve with CHOCOLATE SAUCE on the side. (See Index for recipe.)

Dinner for Four

Foie Gras Frais Cuit Au Torchon

Granite Au Pommard

Supréme of Duck Normamde

Gratin De Fruits Rouge Et Coulis De Frambois

Wines:

With Foie Gras: Sauterne
With Duck: Aloxe Corton
With Gratin: Champagne Brut

Owners: Peabody Court Hotel

Chef: Michele Laudier

CONSERVATORY

Michel J. F. Laudier's spectacular signature has been emblazoned on many fine restaurants, both in his native France where he trained and in the United States. Laudier began his illustrious American career as the chef who established the impeccable reputation of the Rive Gauche during its reign as one of Washington D.C.'s premier dining establishments.

In 1984, when the luxurious 5-★ Peabody Court Hotel opened in Baltimore, Laudier became the executive chef for its elegant conservatory penthouse restaurant and the less formal Brassiere on the ground floor. The spectacular cuisine and the stunning Beaux Arts ambiance of the Conservatory immediately captured the attention of Baltimore's dining-out public, and the restaurant flourished.

When Laudier left the hotel in late 1987, he passed the torch to his talented chef de cuisine, Gilles Monet. Monet, 24, is a graduate of Meuson la Foret in Paris, served as the private chef for the French General staff of the French Air Force, and cooked at l'Etoile d'or in Paris, which rates a star in the Michelin Guide.

Monet supervises a team of five cooks in his spotless, modern kitchen. They are all intensely aware of their responsibility to fulfill the expectations of their clientele in a setting that is decidedly European despite the spectacular view of Baltimore. "We try to create a total atmosphere for a special evening," says Monet, whose mission is supported by maitre-d' Marc Dettori, the restaurant's wine expert.

Monet believes that garniture is an art with a rightful place in food service. Plates are carefully checked before they leave the kitchen, and the food itself looks like a still-life painting upon arrival in front of patrons.

In selecting a menu that best showcases the Conservatory, Monet chose recipes that may be intimidating to the beginner. Yet the quintessential experienced professional chef who despite his years of experience claims that he "discovers something new everyday." It is this freshness of approach and earnest enthusiasm that makes dining at the Conservatory an exciting experience.

Peabody Court Hotel
612 Cathedral Street
Baltimore, Maryland
(301) 727-7101

FOIE GRAS FRAIS CUIT AU TORCHON
Marinated Duck Livers

1st Day:

1. Soak one pound foie gras in lukewarm water for three hours. Open and remove the veins. Soak for one hour in cold water to remove blood. Remove from water and dry.
2. Put it on plate and season it with:

8 grams of salt	*1 pinch nutmeg*
1 pinch white pepper	*Madeira wine sprinkled*
1 teaspoon sugar	*lightly over.*

4. Refrigerate.

2nd Day:

1. Remove from refrigerator. Let sit for one hour.
2. Cover a kitchen towel with parchment paper. Place foie gras on paper. Roll like sausage 3" in diameter and tie at each end. Roll cheesecloth around sausages.
3. Prepare a gallon of chicken stock including one calf's foot. Cook calf's foot in broth for three hours. Strain and return to stock pot.
4. Place foie gras "sausage" in pot. Simmer gently, covered, 25 minutes, then cool quickly. Store in refrigerator overnight.

3rd Day:

Unwrap and re-tighten the cheesecloth bandage. Wait a few hours, then unwrap, slice, and serve with mushrooms and truffles drizzled with sweet almond oil.

Note: M. Laudier uses fresh foie gras from New York state. Not readily available to the average consumer, the fresh product is a signature item at the Conservatory. Tinned foie gras may be substituted. Fresh foie gras is available from A.M. Briggs in Washington, D.C. (202) 832-2600.

GRANITE AU POMMARD
Red wine ice

1/2 bottle of Pommard or red wine   3 ounces sugar
     Juice from 1/2 orange   3 ounces water
     Juice from 1/2 lemon

1. Cook sugar and water together; cool mixture.
2. Stir in red wine and juices.
3. Place in freezer and mix with a fork every two hours. Serve in frozen martini glasses as a palate cleanser.

SUPRÉME OF DUCK NORMANDE

4 breasts of duck, boned   2 ounces of vinegar
    Salt and pepper   1 cup chicken or duck stock
2 tablespoons of clarified butter 1 cup heavy cream
2 apples peeled and cored   1 teaspoon cornstarch
    (save the peel)   1/4 cup Calvados
1/2 cup of sugar   Salt and pepper, to taste

1. Cut apples in half, slice thinly, and shape into fan. Brush with butter, sprinkle with sugar and bake in oven at 350° for 20 minutes.
2. Sauté the duck breasts in clarified butter and cook on each side to medium rare. Put aside.
3. Put 1/2 cup of sugar in a saucepan. Heat to a light caramel color.
4. Add 2 ounces of vinegar. (Be careful not to burn yourself from the steam.) Add peeling of apple to caramelized sugar.
5. Add one cup duck or chicken stock. Cook for five minutes. Add one cup of cream and cook over high heat until reduced by half.

6. Mix cornstarch with a small amount of cold water and add to the sauce to thicken. Finish with a touch of Calvados, salt and pepper.

7. Mix sauce in the blender for a few minutes, then pass it through a fine sieve.

8. Slice your duck breast and put on the plate with 1/2 apple. Nap with sauce. Serve with wild rice and julienne vegetables.

GRATIN DE FRUITS ROUGE ET COULIS DE FRAMBOISE
Raspberry Coulis

1 *pint of raspberry juice*	1/2 *cup raspberry liqueur*
7 *ounces of sugar*	

1. Mix ingredients together in a saucepan.
2. Cook mixture until it has a syrupy consistency.
3. Remove from heat.

Fruits:

1 *pint of strawberries*	1 *pint of raspberries*

1. Slice the strawberries.
2. Arrange them on a platter that will withstand the broiler.
3. Place raspberries in center.

Sauce:

4 *egg yolks*	1/2 *cup of whipped cream*
2 *ounces of sugar*	

1. Beat egg yolks with sugar.
2. Whip the cream and add it to the egg yolks.
3. Cover berries with this sauce.
4. Broil them to a golden brown.
5. Pour the raspberry coulis around the plate.
6. Add fresh mint leaves in the center.

Fritz's

of

Fells Point

Dinner for Four

Goulash Soup

Roast Goose with Red Cabbage

Hunter Style Veal Cutlet in a Mushroom Cream Sauce

Cucumber Salad

Bread Dumplings

Apple Strudel

Wines:

with Veal: Johann Josef. Prüm 1985 - Wehlener Sonnenuhr
with Goose: Davis Bynum, Kabinett
with Dessert: 1983 Piesporter Michelsberg Riesling-Auslese
(Mosel- Saar-Ruwer)

Owner: Fritz Hofer

Manager: Dean Carlson

Chef: Fritz Hofer

FRITZ'S OF FELLS POINT

Travel posters of Germany beckon us with cheery pictures of country inns serving up frothy mugs of cold beer to happy patrons. This seductive image, designed to lure future travelers to the land of sauerbraten, Weiner schnitzel and apple strudel, is closer to home, however, than you may have imagined.

Fritz's of Fells Point has captured not only the ambience of German inns but the essence of German food. Knotty pine tables (try for a cushiony corner banquette), hurricane lamps, antlers of unlucky elks on the walls and German folk music (set at a discreet volume) set the tone for delicious and authentic German food.

Fritz Hofer, proprietor and chef, practiced his craft for twenty years in Austria, Germany and Switzerland. In 1978 he began a three-year stint in Washington, D.C., as executive chef of the Alpenhof restaurant, where he built a fine reputation for the best German food in town. Marriage to a Baltimore woman brought him to our fair city where he resided over Schatze's restaurant kitchen before establishing, Fritz's of Fells Point, in May, 1986.

Fritz is a hard-working, congenial fellow who beams at mention of his success, modestly explaining that he "found the right place at the right time." He is quick to emphasize that his restaurant serves Austrian-German cuisine, which he defines as more complex and refined than simply German food.

Austria is a popular tourist country famous for its resorts that have spawned many fine chefs. Fritz, who trained at the Austria Hotel School, explains that he and his colleagues draw their inspiration from many countries including (northern) Italy, Hungary, Yugoslavia and Germany. Austrian-German food, then, may be labeled with the oft-used word "eclectic," appropriate in this case.

This restaurant's menu, abundant in game and meat dishes (Roast Goose, Pheasant, Leg of Venison, Roast Pork), also takes advantage of its waterfront site, serving fresh Maryland seafood, "prepared according to your choice." Walking through the doors of Fritz's of Fells Point transports you to a fine restaurant in Germany - without the trans-Atlantic fare.

1702 Thames Street, Fells Point
Baltimore, Maryland
(301) 522-4602

GOULASH SOUP

2 onions, chopped
4 ounces (1 stick) margarine
  or butter
1 pound bottom round, cut
  into 1/2-inch cubes
1/4 cup chopped fresh garlic
2 teaspoons marjoram

Salt and fresh ground
  black pepper, to taste
2 teaspoons Hungarian paprika
3 pints water (6 cups)
4 potatoes, peeled and cubed
  Flour and water, to thicken
  Chopped parsley

1. Gently cook the onions in the margarine or butter until tender and translucent.
2. Raise the heat and add the beef cubes, allowing them to brown on all sides. As they are browning, season with the chopped fresh garlic, marjoram, salt, pepper and paprika.
3. Transfer the beef to a stockpot and add water, making certain it just covers the beef. Add the potatoes. Simmer, partially covered, for 45 minutes to one hour or until the beef and potatoes are tender.
4. Adjust seasonings to taste.
5. If soup is too thin, then mix together a little flour and water and add to the simmering mixture until it is of desired consistency. The soup should be rather thick, like a gruel.
6. Pour into individual soup bowls and garnish with chopped parsley.

Note: Although 1/4 cup of chopped garlic may seem extravagant, its strong flavor dissipates as it cooks and actually becomes rather mild.

ROAST GOOSE with RED CABBAGE

1 *8-pound domestic goose*
   Marjoram, to taste
   Salt and fresh ground black
   pepper, to taste
   Hungarian paprika, to taste

1 *large onion, cut into*
   large chunks
1 *celery, cut into large chunks*
1 *carrot, cut into large chunks*
1 *cup red wine*
1 *cup water*

SAUCE:

1 *tablespoon beef or*
   chicken stock base

Flour and water, to thicken

1. Pre-heat the oven to 375°.

2. Remove wing tips from the goose and reserve. Also set aside all of the giblets found inside the goose, washing them well. Pull off excess fat from the cavity of the goose and reserve (for the cabbage). Pull off excess fat found around the legs of the goose. Wash the goose well.

3. Season the goose healthily with marjoram, salt, pepper and paprika, inside and out. Place in a large roasting pan, strewing the reserved wing tips, giblets, onions, celery and carrots around it.

4. Pour the red wine and water around the goose.

5. Roast, covered, in the pre-heated 375° oven for approximately 1 1/2 hours, pouring off the excess fat every half hour.

6. Remove goose to a serving platter. Strain the liquid into a saucepan. Add the beef or chicken stock base and heat on top of the stove until simmering. Mix together flour and water and add enough to the simmering sauce that it thickens slightly. The end result should be a "pourable gravy."

7. Carve the goose and serve with the gravy and red cabbage.

Note: Serves 6 to 8

RED CABBAGE

2 heads red cabbage	1 cup sugar
1 onion, chopped	3/4 teaspoons nutmeg
1/2 cup raisins (optional)	Salt and fresh black pepper, to taste
1/2 cup sautéed chopped bacon	
1 cup red wine	Reserved rendered drippings from the goose
3 apples, peeled and chopped	
1 cup wine vinegar	2 cups beef stock, if necessary

1. Wash and shred the cabbage. Place in a stockpot.

2. Add all remaining ingredients except the beef stock. Simmer over a low heat, covered, for approximately 1 1/2 hours, stirring occasionally.

3. If the cabbage mixture appears to be getting too thick then thin with beef stock, as needed.

HUNTER STYLE VEAL CUTLET
in a MUSHROOM CREAM SAUCE

1 1/4 pounds boneless veal cutlet, pounded to 1/4-inch (figure 5 ounces per person)	1/2 pound quartered mushrooms
	Brandy
	White wine
Salt and fresh ground black pepper, to taste	1/2 cup DEMI-GLACE SAUCE (see Index for recipe)
Hungarian paprika	
Flour, for dredging	1/2 cup table cream or half and half
2-3 ounces margarine or butter	
4 ounces bacon, chopped	1/3 cup chopped parsley
1 small onion, chopped	

1. Season the meat with salt, pepper and paprika. Just before sautéing, dredge in flour, shaking off the excess.

2. Sauté in hot margarine or butter until brown on each side, about 30 seconds per side. Drain pan of extra fat.

3. With veal still in the pan, add bacon, onion and mushrooms, continuing to cook for 2-3 minutes longer.

4. Add a splash of brandy and a splash of white wine.

5. Add the Demi-Glace Sauce to the pan along with the cream or half and half. Allow to reduce for several minutes. Add the chopped parsley and let the sauce simmer until it has achieved the proper consistency. Serve.

Note: This veal dish calls for the veal to be pounded to 1/4-inch thickness at the very least. Do not pound it as thin as you would for scallopine or else it will overcook in this particular recipe.

CUCUMBER SALAD

2 medium cucumbers
Salt
White pepper, to taste
1/3 cup white vinegar

1/2 tablespoons chopped fresh garlic
1 cup sour cream

1. Peel the cucumbers and slice very thinly.

2. Place the cucumbers in a colander, sprinkle with salt and drain for several hours. Pat dry.

3. Season to taste with white pepper.

4. Add the white vinegar and garlic.

5. Gently blend in the sour cream. Serve.

Note: This dish is best made ahead of time to allow the flavors to mellow.

BREAD DUMPLINGS

5 slices bacon, fried,
   drained and minced

3 cups 1/2-inch stale bread cubes
   (about 8 thick slices)

3 tablespoons finely
   minced onion

1/4 cup flour

1/4 teaspoon salt
   White pepper, to taste

1/2 teaspoon marjoram

2 tablespoons minced chives

1/2 cup milk

2 large eggs, well beaten

1. Mix together all of the dry ingredients, then stir in the milk and beaten eggs. Allow to sit for 10 minutes.
2. Re-mix and then form into 2-inch balls. Dust lightly with flour.
3. Bring a large pot of water to a boil and reduce heat until water is just simmering. Drop in the dumplings and simmer, uncovered, for 7 or 8 minutes.
4. Remove from water with a slotted spoon. Serve with available pan juices or sauce over the dumplings. Yields 8 dumplings.

Note: These dumplings are excellent in soups and stews as well. For these, make smaller dumplings and reduce cooking time to 5 minutes. It is important that the water only simmers and never boils or else the dumplings will be very tough.

Yields 8 dumplings.

APPLE STRUDEL

Homemade or commercial
   puff pastry sheets
4 apples, unpeeled and
   finely chopped
2/3 cup sugar
1 tablespoon cinnamon

1/2 cup dark raisins
1/2 cup fine, dried breadcrumbs
1/4 cup dark rum
2 egg yolks, beaten

GARNISH:

Powdered sugar   Lightly whipped cream

1. Grease well a small sheet pan (cookie sheet with sides).
2. Place the apples in a bowl and add sugar and cinnamon, mixing well.
3. Blend in the raisins.
4. Add the dried breadcrumbs and rum, blending all ingredients together well.
5. Roll out the puff pastry on a floured surface to a rectangle that is slightly larger than the sheet pan itself. If you are using commercial sheets of puff pastry, allow them to soften a bit before rolling.
6. Place the apple mixture in a fat cigar down the length of the pastry, leaving a 1 1/2-inch margin on each short end.
7. Starting from the long end nearest you, roll the strudel up tightly. Place seam side down on the prepared sheet pan.
8. Brush all over with the egg yolk. Turn the two short ends over on themselves to form a seal. Brush again with the egg yolk.
9. Poke small holes with a fork all along the length of the strudel in order for steam to escape.
10. Bake in a preheated 375° oven for 20-25 minutes or until golden brown. Dust with powdered sugar. Cut into pieces and serve with lightly whipped cream.

Serves 6-8.

**HARBOR COURT
HOTEL**

Dinner for Four

Escargot in Roasted Garlic Sauce

Veal Chop with Shitake Mushrooms and Port Sauce

Belgian Endive Curls with Roquefort Cheese

Almond Lace Baskets with Grand Marnier Strawberries

Wines:

Paul Roger Blanc De Chardonnay, 1979
Congress Springs Cabernet Franc, 1984
Loire Valley Pouilly-Fume Paviot, 1985
Quady Essensia
(A California dessert wine made with orange Muscat grapes)

Owners: Harbor Court Hotel

Chef: Michael York

HAMPTON'S AT HARBOR COURT

Seated comfortably in the lap of luxury, those who come to dine at Hampton's in the Harbor Court Hotel are amply rewarded. While classical music plays unobtrusively in the background and a maitre-d' hovers equally unobtrusively in the wings, guests enjoy impeccable service with food and wine to match in surroundings that both soothe and stimulate.

The spacious, high-ceilinged room is furnished in the style of a formal family dining room at the turn of the century. Antique sideboards, upholstered chairs, wall sconces, and table lamps contribute to the comfortable atmosphere. Waiters in black-tie are knowledgeable about both food and wine, and so are the clientele. Hampton's is a celebratory kind of place, ideal for special occasions or family gatherings as well as an intimate tête-à-tête.

Hampton's chef, Michael York, has been cooking for fifteen of his thirty-eight years. After studying at the Culinary Institute of America in New-York, York worked at various restaurants and country clubs in New England before becoming a chef-partner in Tony's, a five-star restaurant in Houston, Texas. Since arriving in Baltimore to open the dining rooms at Harbor Court (including the hotel's more casual Cafe Brighton), York has established a solid reputation as one of the city's most innovative chefs.

Hampton's menu reflects his grasp of classic cuisine as well as his ability to stage culinary fireworks with such items as escargots in roasted garlic sauce, crab-stuffed pears poached in pear liqueur with a mousseline glaze, and entrees ranging from blackened buffalo steaks with a mushroom-shallot marmalade to red snapper sauced with a blend of leeks and vermouth.

Wines are a strong suit at Hampton's where the wine list reflects the astute judgement of sommelier Philip Bernot. Attention to every amenity of ambience and nuance of service paired with superb food make Hampton's one of Baltimore's finest first-class restaurants.

Harbor Court Hotel
550 Light Street
Baltimore, Maryland
(301) 234-0550

ESCARGOT IN ROASTED GARLIC SAUCE

24 escargots
2 quarts of whipping cream
1/2 teaspoon of chicken base
1/2 teaspoon thyme
1/2 teaspoon of ground black pepper

1/2 cup fresh basil, minced
1/2 bulb garlic
4 ounces Madeira wine
1-1/2 ounces fontina cheese
Salt and pepper, to taste

1. Reduce cream by half by simmering on stove.
2. Place garlic in oven until lightly browned; peel garlic after roasting. Chop finely.
3. Add wine and seasonings; simmer 5 minutes. Add cheese and simmer until cheese melts. Add escargots. Heat through.

Note: Escargots are available in tins in specialty shops or gourmet section. Small cans hold about 24.

JULIENNE VEGETABLES

1 zucchini
1 red pepper

1 sheet of puff pastry
Fresh basil for garnish

1. Peel whole zucchini and cut into one inch lengths; slice like matchsticks.
2. Roast large red pepper at 350° for 10-15 minutes until brown. Peel; discard skin. (Skin will tear easily when roasted). Seed, and cut into thin strips.
3. Remove one sheet of puff pastry from box. Cut in half. Beat one egg, and wet top of one sheet of puff pastry. Place another sheet on top. Use cookie cutter to cut eight rounds. Line cookie sheet with parchment paper. Brush tops of shapes with egg mixture. Bake at 350° for 8-10 minutes, or until golden brown.

Assembly: Line individual bowls with julienne vegetables. Place snails on top, spoon sauce over. Arrange two puff pastry shells on either side. Garnish with fresh basil.

Note: Puff pastry is located in the frozen food section of most supermarkets.

BRAISED VEAL CHOP WITH
SHITAKE MUSHROOMS AND PORT SAUCE

4 center cut rib veal chops	3 ounces butter
Flour to dredge chops	1 pint heavy cream
Salt and pepper	8 ounces veal stock
6 ounces washed & sliced	1/4 cup of Ruby Port wine
shitake mushrooms	Chopped parsley

1. Trim and season veal chops with salt and pepper, then dredge in flour.

2. Over moderate heat sauté veal chops in butter until golden brown on both sides. Then bake in oven at 350° for 15 minutes until pink or medium. Do not overcook.

3. Remove chops from skillet.

4. Add wine, deglaze pan. Boil to reduce; add cream. Boil again to reduce by 1/2. Add veal stock and continue to reduce until thick.

5. Add parsley, salt, pepper and mushrooms. Put sauce over veal chops and serve immediately.

BELGIAN ENDIVE CURLS WITH ROQUEFORT CHEESE

2 whole Belgian endive	8 tablespoons basil vinegar
8 ounces Roquefort cheese	1/4 cup chopped walnuts
1/4 cup walnut oil	Pinch of black pepper

1. Cut off ends of the endive and separate leaves, leaving center core whole. Blend roquefort cheese with pepper to taste in blender until smooth . With knife, spread cheese mixture into leaves about 1/4 inch thick.

2. When completely stuffed, place them together to form the original shape of the endive starting with the smaller leaves toward center and larger ones on the outside. Then wrap together with plastic wrap to hold them together. Refrigerate for about 1 hour or until firm.

3. To prepare dressing blend oil, vinegar, pepper and walnuts together.

4. Unwrap endive and slice about 1/4" thick. Arrange on plates (two per serving). Put sauce around curls and garnish with sliced apple or parsley sprigs.

ALMOND LACE BASKETS WITH
GRAND MARNIER STRAWBERRIES

4 ounces of butter

6 ounces of sugar

4 ounces of corn syrup

4 ounces of bread flour

4 ounces of blanched almonds

2 pints strawberries

1 cup Grand Marnier

Mint liquer (optional)

1. Cook butter, sugar and corn syrup over low heat to blend together. Add 4 ounces of bread flour, mix well, cook 10 minutes. Take off fire, add 4 ounces of blanched almonds. Let cool to room temperature.

2. Cut parchment paper to make 5x5 squares; place some of the mixture (about the size of a golf ball) into the middle of the squares. Bake at 400° in the oven for 15 minutes until golden brown. Remove from oven and cool for 1-1/2 minutes (no longer). With spatula, remove and arrange on top of a coffee cup to form a basket. Let cool on cup and carefully remove.

Strawberries

Wash and slice 2 pints of strawberries. Place in bowl with 1 cup of Grand Marnier. Add 1/2 cup of sugar; let sit for 2 hours. Put into baskets and serve with fresh whipped cream splashed with mint liquor or Grand Marnier. Garnish with mint leaves.

Restaurant, Inc.

Dinner for Four

Strawberry Soup

Grilled Salmon Kebobs

Lemon Rice

Cheese Bread

Baked Brie in Puff Pastry with Beurre Chambord Sauce

Wines:

with the Salmon:
Alderbrook Chardonnay, 1985 (Dry Creek Valley)
or Pouilly Fume Les Pechignolles, 1985 (Gitton)
with the Dessert:
Joseph Phelps, 1985 Late Harvest Riesling

Proprietor: Mrs. Frances Haussner

Manager: Stephen George

HAUSSNER'S RESTUARANT

Nowhere has Baltimore's urban renaissance of the past decade been more apparent than in the proliferation of superb dining establishments. These new restaurants which have placed our city on the culinary map can tip their hats (or chef's toques!) to their forebears.

Haussner's Restaurant is one of Baltimore's proudest success stories. Owned and operated by the same family for over 50 years now, Haussner's is a local landmark and an internationally acclaimed dining establishment, known for both its cuisine and awesome art collection.

Frances Haussner, owner, is an avid art collector and a walk through Haussner's is not unlike a walk through a museum! Every conceivable space is filled with paintings, bronzes, wood carvings, etchings -- not for sale, merely for the pleasure of you, the diner, and of course, Mrs. Haussner and her family.

The management of Haussner's is now under the tutelage of her daughter and son-in-law, Mr. and Mrs. Stephen George. Mrs. George credits much of Haussner's success to the longevity of key employees, many of whom have been there for over 40 years. One of the kitchen managers has been with them for 32 years and he's only 46 years old!

Haussner's is not merely a large restaurant, it is a huge one. The main dining room accommodates 500, the upstairs banquet rooms seat 30 and 100, the new downstairs lounge seats 225. Two-thousand meals are served daily from an enormous menu emphasizing seafood preparations and classic German food prepared to order.The downstairs lounge relies on "grazing style" food such as St. Louis Spareribs and Buffalo Chicken Wings. (It also has live entertainment and dancing!)

How then to explain the excellence of the food? Haussner's employs over two dozen day and night cooks that are fortunate to be working in a fantastic state-of-the-art kitchen. The famous bakery has moved to an off-premise site; Haussner's baked goods are now sold in several retail food stores throughout the Baltimore metropolitan area.

This blend of efficient use of working space, loyal and hard-working employees,"respect for customers and pride in product" has made Haussner's the smashing success story it is today.

3242 Eastern Avenue
Baltimore, Maryland
(301) 327-8365

STRAWBERRY SOUP

1 pint strawberries	1/4 cup honey
2 cups yogurt	1 ounce Strawberry Schnapps
1/2 cup sour cream	

1. Wash and cap the strawberries. Reserve 4 for garnish.

2. Place all ingredients in a food processor. Purée until the mixture is smooth and creamy. Refrigerate until chilled and thickened, about 2-3 hours.

3. Serve very cold. Garnish with strawberry slices and a dollop of sour cream.

Note: If you do not have Strawberry Schnapps you may substitute Amaretto or an orange-flavored liqueur such as Grand Marnier or Cointreau.

GRILLED SALMON KEBOBS

3 pounds fresh salmon steaks	16 firm cherry tomatoes
1 medium green pepper	1 bottle creamy italian salad dressing
1 medium mild white onion	
16 medium-sized fresh mushrooms	8 metal skewers

1. Remove bones from salmon steaks. Cut remaining fillets with skin on into 24 pieces.

2. Wash and core the green pepper. Cut into halves then each half into 8 pieces. Repeat this procedure with the onion. Clean and remove stems from mushrooms. Leave cherry tomatoes whole.

3. Thread the following on 1 metal skewer, arranging for effective color: 3 salmon pieces, 2 onion chunks, 2 green pepper chunks, 2 mushrooms and 2 tomatoes. Repeat procedure with remaining 7 metal skewers.

4. Place completed skewers in a shallow baking pan. Marinate with Italian dressing for at least 3 hours in the refrigerator. Remove kebobs to a broiler pan. Broil under high heat until fish is cooked.

5. Serve two kebobs on a bed of SEASONED RICE (recipe follows).

Note: This is an excellent summertime outdoor-grill recipe. Try adding mesquite or hickory wood chips to your charcoal for great flavor!

SEASONED LEMON RICE

1 cup long-grain rice
1 teaspoon lemon dill herb mix
   Pinch of white pepper

Juice from 1 lemon
1 lemon, cut in 8 wedges
   to garnish

Cook rice according to package directions. Mix with lemon dill herb mix, pepper and lemon juice.

CHEESE BREAD

2 cups water
1 ounce dry yeast
3-4 tablespoons sugar
1/2 ounce shortening

1-2 teaspoons salt
10 ounce grated Cheddar cheese
4 cups bread flour or all-purpose
   Dash garlic powder

1. Sprinkle yeast over 1/2 cup of the warm water, add half of the sugar and stir to dissolve with a spoon or fork. In approximately 7-10 minutes the yeast/water mixture should be very bubbly. This procedure proves that the yeast is viable. Once the yeast is working, add the remaining water and sugar. Transfer to a large bowl.

2. Add remaining ingredients, mixing well with a wooden spoon until mixture is well blended and smooth. You may want to transfer the dough to a lightly floured board and knead it for several minutes to achieve the consistency you desire.

3. Place dough in a lightly greased bowl and let it rise until it is doubled in bulk. Test this by inserting two fingers into the dough to make a 1" depression. If the depression immediately fills up again with dough, the bread is not sufficiently risen; if the depression remains in the dough, then the bread has risen enough. Depending upon the temperature of your kitchen, this first rising will take approximately 1 hour.

4. Shape the dough into two loaves and transfer to two bread pans. Let rise again until puffy, approximately 45 more minutes.

5. Bake in a preheated 375° oven for 35-40 minutes or until the bottom of the loaf sounds hollow when tapped with your knuckles.

Note: Recipe may require additional flour if all-purpose is used.

BAKED BRIE IN PUFF PASTRY
with BEURRE CHAMBORD SAUCE

1 *pound puff pastry or QUICK
   PUFF PASTRY (recipe follows)*
2 *4-ounce mini Brie cheeses*

Fresh raspberries to garnish
*BEURRE CHAMBORD
   SAUCE (recipe follows)*

1. Roll the puff pastry out to a 1/4" thick rectangle. Cut 8 3" squares from the dough. Place 4 of those squares on an ungreased cookie sheet. Cut out a 2" square from the center of the 4 remaining squares leaving, a 1/2" wide picture frame. Brush edges of bottom squares with a soft brush that has been dipped in water. Carefully place picture frames on bottom squares and press lightly. Bake at 400° for 15 minutes. Remove from oven. When cool, cut out the inside center of each square leaving an opening.
2. Remove all rind from each wheel of Brie. Cut each wheel into 4 equal triangular pieces. Place 2 pieces, outside edges together to form a square, in each baked puff pastry square. Broil on an ungreased cookie sheet on bottom oven rack position just until cheese is soft and glazed.
3. Divide Beurre Chambord among 4 room temperature plates. Place a warm baked Brie on each. Garnish with raspberries.

QUICK PUFF PASTRY

FLOUR PACKAGE:

2 1/2 *cups all-purpose flour*
   3 *tablespoons cold butter,
     cut into pieces*
   1 *teaspoon salt*

1/2 *cup plus 1 tablespoon
   cold water*
  1 *egg yolk*

BUTTER PACKAGE:

1 1/2 cups flour   *1 pound minus the 3*
                                       tablespoons cold butter, cut
                                       into 1/2" cubes

1. For the flour package: Place the flour and butter in the container of a food processor.With the steel blade in place process for 2-3 seconds until a coarse meal forms. Mix together the water, salt and egg yolk. With the processor running, pour the water mixture through the feed tube in a fast, steady stream until the mixture just comes together into a ball of dough (10-15 seconds). Remove dough, form into a disk, wrap and refrigerate while you work with the butter.

2. For the butter package: In the container of a food processor mix the butter and flour together until the entire mass looks like all butter. Remove from container and form into a square.

3. Remove the flour package from the refrigerator. Form an "X" halfway down. Open up and pull down the four "petals." Roll them out with even strokes until they are about 8" long or enough to enclose the square of butter completely. A small portion of the center of the dough should not be touched as you roll and should result in a slightly raised platform about 1" high. Upon this platform place the butter square. Fold over the "petals" to secure the butter inside; be sure it is sealed in with no holes. Pinch the edges together. Sprinkle the top lightly with flour and turn it upside down. Sprinkle your work surface lightly with flour.

4. First and Second Rolls ("turns") - Roll the dough into a rectangle somewhere around 8" wide by 18" long. Use long even strokes, moving in one direction only and stopping to within 1" of either end. Once you have achieved the required length and width of dough, roll over the ends once or twice to thin them. Never push down too hard or you will squeeze the layers together and the dough will not rise as high. Brush off excess flour. Fold both ends to an imaginary center line and then fold one on top of the other. This constitutes a "double turn."

Lightly flatten the folds with the palms of your hands to make the dough of even thickness. Rotate the dough so the short edge faces you and the long side is open at the right, like a book. Roll out again to the same 8" x 18" rectangle and fold and turn again. Wrap and refrigerate for 15-20 minutes.

5. Third and Fourth Rolls ("turns") - Roll out once again to an 8" x 18" rectangle. Brush off excess flour, give the pastry a "double turn" and rotate the dough. Repeat for the fourth, and last, roll and turn.

6. Refrigerate for 30 minutes before rolling out and forming. If you must refrigerate it for several hours or overnight, bring it out to room temperature and let it warm and soften a bit for 30-60 minutes.

Note: In a pinch you may use frozen puff pastry sheets.

BEURRE CHAMBORD SAUCE

3/4 cup dry white wine	1/4 pound unsalted butter
2 medium shallots, minced	(1 stick), softened
1/2 cup minus 2 tablespoons whipping cream	2 ounces Chambord (raspberry liqueur)

1. Boil wine and shallots in a small heavy saucepan, reducing liquid to about 3 tablespoons. Strain into a clean saucepan, pressing liquid from shallots.

2. Add cream and reduce to half.

3. Remove pan from heat and whisk in the butter, adding it in batches until a smooth emulsion is formed. Alternate moving the saucepan on and off of the heat so that the butter additions remain warm, but not so hot that the emulsion breaks down. If the sauce does break (the butter melts and rises to the top), then whisk in 1 tablespoon of cold butter to bring it back.

4. Add Chambord and whisk until blended.

IKAROS

Dinner for Six

*Classical Greek Eggplant Salad
with Pita Bread*

Avgolemono Soup with Rice

Shrimp Guvetski

Baklava

Greek Coffee

Cafe Ikaros

Wines:

*Achaia-Clauss Retsina
St. Rosa Rose St. Helena White Wine
Acacia Clauss Mavro Daphne of Patras (Dessert wine)*

Owners: Theodossios and Xenos Kohilas

Chef: Theodossios Kohilas

Ikaros

Whitewashed walls and a bright blue awning identify Ikaros, Baltimore's favorite Greek restaurant in the eastern section of the city. Established in 1969 by brothers Theodossios and Xenos Kohilas, Ikaros is named after their native Island of Ikaria and authentically represents a typical taverna.

One comes here for a feeling of the old country as well as for food that would be familiar to any resident of Athens. Chef Theodossios cooked at the famous Pantheon and Corfu restaurants in that Greek metropolis before coming to this country nearly 20 years ago. He has recently returned from an extended visit to his homeland, during which Xenos ran the restaurant with a gentle but sure hand.

Xenos is an artist at heart. His own impressionistic-style paintings are among the many art works that adorn the walls of the 247 seat restaurant. Mural-sized scenes of sunny Greek villages as well as a classic rendition of the Parthenon are reminders of the restaurant's roots. Greek music on the sound system adds to the atmosphere. A wine cellar in the foyer is filled with Greek wines, and among the loyal patrons who come from Washington, D.C., are many local people for whom Ikaros is a friendly neighborhood restaurant.

Lamb is braised, baked, roasted, and grilled (as only the Greeks know how) by Theodossios and his staff. Specialties of the kitchen include whole flounder and sea bass "broiled the Ikaros way" with a hint of olive oil and a lemon sauce, as well as octopus prepared with rosé wine, and feta cheese and seafood in phyllo. Chef Theodossios favors oregano, lemon, and garlic in his cooking -- flavors that make his food sing with the distinctive flavors of Greek cuisine. The kitchen is stocked with tins of Greek olive oil and the freshest of feta cheese, key ingredients for many of his recipes.

Ikaros is a family-run restaurant, one steeped in the traditions of the old country. The Kohilas family traces its roots to the Island of Crete in the 1600s, and has a dated document marking the family's migration to Ikaria in 1746. They have preserved the Greek spirit in a remarkable way, and share it with all who come here for a taste of the past as well as for good food cooked as it has been for many centuries.

4805 Eastern Avenue
Baltimore, Maryland
(301) 633-3750

CLASSICAL GREEK EGGPLANT SALAD

2 *large eggplants*	3 *cloves of garlic, minced*
2 *tablespoons of parsley, chopped*	1/4 *cup of oil*
4 *tablespoons of mayonnaise*	*Salt and pepper, to taste*
3 *tablespoons of vinegar*	*Pita bread*
1 *small onion, grated*	

1. Bake whole eggplants at 350° for one hour or until soft.

2. Remove from oven, dip in cold water and peel skin; discard.

3. Dice eggplant and place in a bowl. Add onion, garlic, parsley, mayonnaise, oil, vinegar, and season to taste.

4. Stir well and let stand one hour before serving.

5. Garnish with Greek olives and serve as a spread with warmed pita bread cut into quarters.

CHICKEN AVGOLEMONO SOUP WITH RICE

2-3 *pounds of chicken*	1 *teaspoon parsley*
2-1/2 *quarts of water*	1/2 *cup uncooked rice*
2 *stalks of celery, sliced*	3 *eggs*
1 *carrot, chopped*	*Juice of 1-1/2 - 2 lemons*
1 *medium onion, chopped*	*Salt and pepper, to taste*
1 *teaspoon thyme*	

1. Place chicken in pot covered with water, bring to a boil, and cook an additional 15 minutes. Skim surface. Add the vegetables and simmer 1-1/2 hours. Remove the chicken and strain stock. Discard vegetables. When chicken is cool, skin and de-bone and cut into bite-sized pieces. Return chicken to broth, add rice, and cook 15-20 minutes or until rice is cooked to your liking.

2. In a bowl add eggs and lemon juice; beat until frothy. Slowly add 3 cups of the soup to egg mixture, stirring to avoid curdling. Return this mixture to the main soup, and stir. Garnish with chopped parsley and serve immediately.

SHRIMP GUVETSKI

1-1/2 pounds of shrimp peeled and
     deveined (use 16-20 count)
1-1/2 pounds of feta cheese
  2 beef bouillon cubes
  1 pound of orzo
  5 cups of water
  2 tablespoons of butter

1 onion, chopped
1 clove of garlic, minced
  oregano
1 8-ounce can of tomato sauce
1/2 cup of rose wine
  Salt and pepper, to taste

1. Pour five cups of water into a heavy oven-proof pan. Add onion, garlic, beef buillon cubes, oregano, salt, pepper and butter.

2. Place in oven at 450° and allow to boil. Add wine and tomato sauce and lower to 350°. Allow to simmer. Meanwhile parboil orzo in salted water for five minutes.

3. Drain well and add to sauce in roasting pan. Stir well and bake another 15 minutes. While orzo is cooking, boil shrimp for 2 minutes.

4. Transfer orzo to individual ramekins or large casserole dish that may be brought to the table for serving.

5. Add the shrimp to the orzo, top with slices of feta cheese and return to oven until the feta is almost melted or until the orzo is the consistency of cooked rice.

Note: Orzo is a Greek pasta, available in specialty food sections of most supermarkets.

BAKLAVA

3	cups coarsely chopped English walnuts	1 to 1-1/2	cups unsalted butter, melted
1 to 2	teaspoons ground cinnamon	1/4 to 1	pound phyllo pastry
1/2	teaspoon ground cloves		SUGAR SYRUP (see below)

1. Combine the nuts with the cinnamon and cloves.

2. Brush a 3" deep baking pan with melted butter. Place a sheet of phyllo dough in the baking pan and brush well with the melted butter. Stack another 7 sheets one by one on top of the first, brushing each with warm melted butter as you stack it.

3. Sprinkle a handful of the nuts evenly over the dough. Take 2 more phyllo sheets from the package. Place 1 sheet at a time on the nut mixture; brush each with warm melted butter. Sprinkle evenly with another handful of the nut mixture.

4. Repeat this layering process until all nuts are used. Then layer the remaining phyllo sheets, brushing each with warm melted butter, until you have used all the sheets. Make sure that the final sheet is brushed very well with butter.

5. Press around the inside of the pan with your fingers to seal the edges of the sheets. Using a sharp, serrated knife, cut across the width of the pan at 2" intervals, then cut diagonally to make diamond shapes.

6. Place pan on top shelf in a 325° oven and bake 35-40 minutes or until pastry is a deep brown, crisp and cooked through. Let cool about 30 minutes.

7. While the baklava is cooking, make the SUGAR SYRUP. Pour hot syrup over partially cooled baklava. It will absorb the syrup. Let cool and serve.

Note: Phyllo pastry is similar to strudel dough. It is available frozen in many gourmet markets or in Mediterranean groceries. The sheets are paper-thin and must be covered with a damp cloth so they do not dry out as you are working with them. Regardless of recipe, the procedure is always the same; that is, the leaves are brushed copiously with melted butter. Choose a pan the size of the phyllo, or cut the phyllo to fit the pan. This recipe serves 12 to 14 people. Baklava keeps for well over a week in a covered container.

The flavor of baklava is even better the next day.

SUGAR SYRUP

This, too, may be made in quantity and kept in a bottle on a shelf for many weeks.

1-1/2 *cups sugar*	1/2 *cup honey*
1-1/2 *cups water*	*Grated rind of 1 lemon*
3 *whole cloves*	1 *teaspoon vanilla extract*
1 *cinnamon stick*	

1. Combine the sugar, water, cloves and cinnamon stick. Bring to a boil. Simmer for 2 minutes.

2. Add honey and lemon rind, boiling for 5 minutes. Skim the froth.

3. Remove from the heat and discard the cloves and cinnamon stick. Stir in the vanilla extract.

Note: Make sure your sugar has dissolved in the water before you attempt to boil the syrup or it will crystallize.

GREEK COFFEE

1-1/2 *cups water*   *Sugar to taste*
   6 *heaping teaspoons Greek coffee*
       (available in specialty
       shops)

1. Heat water in a pot until hot but not boiling. Dissolve Greek coffee (1 teaspoon per cup) in the water. Add sugar to taste (usually 1/2 teaspoon per cup is sufficient).

2. Let the coffee come up just to the boiling point. When it just begins to rise up in the pot, remove from the heat. Do not boil.

3. Take some of the strong residue that rises to the top of the pot and place it in each cup. Add remaining coffee. This coffee is very strong and excellent with Baklava.

CAFE IKAROS

To an American-sized cup of freshly brewed Greek coffee, add 1/2 ounce each of ouzo, Greek brandy, Kahlúa, and Tia Maria. Add whipped cream if desired.

Baltimore's Famous

Obrycki's

Dinner for Four

Obrycki's Tuna Chowder

Broiled Stuffed Crab

Rose's Coleslaw

*Eclairs Supreme
with Chocolate Sauce*

Wines:

*Boordy Premium White
(Fruity White Wine from One of Maryland's Oldest Vineyards)*

Owners/Operators: Rose and Richard Cernak

Chef: John Bacon III

OBRYCKI'S

If there is a single typically-Baltimore restaurant, OBrycki's is it. Opened as a restaurant in 1944, OBrycki's original premises are in a townhouse built in 1851, and the main dining rooms are located on the site of a tavern established in 1865. Owner-operators Rose and Richard Cernak and their family have been greeting customers since 1976, when they bought the restaurant and began carving out the friendly identity OBrycki's enjoys today.

The Cernak's five children and two of their spouses share responsibilities of Rose and Richard. Mrs. Cernak is the mood-setter of the mellow Fells Point crabhouse, although she calls her husband "the big thinker who pushes us to expansion." When New York City's American Festival Cafe invited the Cernaks to put on a typical Baltimore crab feast at their Rockefeller Plaza restaurant, it was so successful, that it is now an annual event.

Maryland crab, the sweetest of all, is served at the restaurant in-season (June through late fall). Crabs from Florida, Louisiana, and North Carolina are used to keep the restaurant running year-round. "Florida soft crab are wonderful; their hard crabs tend to be light," says Mr. Cernak. From January until mid-May, the restaurant is open weekends only, serving a limited menu of crab soup and steamed crabs. "We're in full bloom from July until December," says he, noting that during these months it is best to make reservations even on weekdays.

Located in a typical Baltimore neighborhood, the restaurant is centered with an equally typical Baltimore bar. Presided over by son Ricki, inventor of the fruity, liquor-laced house drink "Obrycki Ricki," this comfortable bar mellows fellow-patrons as soon as they walk in the door.

An old church pew in the foyer sets the tone for a newly-redecorated interior where brick archways, handsome old stained-glass windows, and flowered wallpaper have been artfully used to suggest the stability for which Obrycki's is known. When asked about "return business," Mrs. Cernak wanted the question refined. "Do you mean how many times a week or a month?" she asked seriously, noting that the group who had just left had come back for a third time in a single week. Obrycki's feels like home.

1727-29 East Pratt Street
Baltimore, Maryland
(301) 732-6305

OBRYCKI'S TUNA CHOWDER

16 *ounces tuna packed in oil*	2 *chicken bouillon cubes*
1 *cup potatoes, boiled,*	2 1/2 *slices white American cheese*
diced and reserved	1 *bay leaf*
1/2 *tablespoon bacon fat*	1/4 *teaspoon thyme*
1/2 *tablespoon butter*	*Salt, to taste*
1 1/2 *cups chopped onion*	*White pepper, to taste*
1 *cup chopped celery*	1 *cup half-and-half*
2 1/4 *tablespoons flour*	1/2 *cup milk*
1 1/4 *cups water*	

1. Drain oil from tuna. Add oil to bacon fat and butter and sauté onion and celery in this mixture for about five minutes.

2. Sprinkle with flour and stir well. Add water, bouillon cubes, and sliced cheese, stirring until cheese is melted.

3. Add bay leaf, thyme, salt and pepper. Bring to a boil and simmer for 15 minutes. Discard bay leaf, add tuna, potatoes, half-and-half, and milk. Heat thoroughly without boiling. Serves 4.

OBRYCKI'S BROILED STUFFED CRAB

4 *JUMBO hard shell crabs, steamed*	1 *cup mayonnaise*
1 *pound lump or backfin crab meat*	*Juice of 1/2 lemon*
1 *egg yolk*	*Paprika*

1. After crabs have steamed and cooled, remove the apron from the crabs, discarding the intestines and fat, and leaving the yellow mustard. With a knife that has a sharp point, remove the top membrane of the crab, so that the crab meat is accessible.

2. Mix together egg yolk, mayonnaise, and lemon. Reserve 1/4 cup mayonnaise. Mix rest of mayonnaise with crab meat and place one-fourth of the mixture on top of each cleaned crab, smoothing and rounding it gently.

3. With a spatula, spread mayonnaise over crab meat mixture. Sprinkle with paprika. Broil until golden brown, and serve with a lemon wedge and drawn butter. Serves 4.

ROSE'S COLE SLAW

8 cups shredded white cabbage
1 cup mayonnaise
1/4 cup white vinegar
1/4 cup white sugar

1 teaspoon salt
1 tablespoon chopped onion
1/4 cup grated carrots

Mix together all ingredients except cabbage. When blended, toss with cabbage and refrigerate until ready to serve. Serves 6.

ECLAIRS SUPREME

PUFF PASTRY (recipe below)
Vanilla ice cream
CHOCOLATE SAUCE
 (recipe follows)

English walnut pieces
Shredded coconut
Maraschino cherries

PUFF PASTRY FOR ECLAIRS
(Makes 10-12 shells)

A secret to perfect puff pastry making is to slit the shells when you remove them from the oven, and then remove the uncooked centers. The shells should be firm to the touch, lightly browned, and crisp. Puff shells freeze well. Just before using frozen shells, place in 425° oven to thaw and crisp them.

1 cup water
3 ounces butter, cut into pieces
1 teaspoon salt
1/8 teaspoon vanilla

1 teaspoon sugar
Pinch of nutmeg
1 cup sifted all-purpose flour
4 large eggs

1. Bring water to a boil in heavy bottomed saucepan. Add butter and seasonings, stirring to melt butter.

2. Remove pan from heat and dump in flour all at once. Beat until flour is thoroughly blended.

3. Over medium heat, beat vigorously with a wooden spoon until mixture separates from the sides of the pan and forms a mass in the middle of the pot.

4. Remove pan from heat, and make an indentation in the middle of the mass. Break an egg into the center of the well, and beat until absorbed. Repeat the procedure with each of the remaining eggs. When mixture is smooth and glossy, use pastry bag fitted with a large plain tip to pipe pastry onto greased cookie sheets. Space oblong mounds 2 inches apart, and brush with mixture of 1/2 teaspoon water and 1 egg beaten together.

5. Bake for 20 minutes in 425°oven. Reduce heat to 375° and bake for 10 more minutes. Remove from oven, make 1-inch slit in sides, and return to oven (leaving door ajar) for 10 minutes. Remove from oven, slit eclairs in half, and remove damp centers. Cool or refreeze.

6. When ready to serve, fill with vanilla ice cream, and drizzle with CHOCOLATE SAUCE. Sprinkle with shredded coconut and walnuts, and top with cherry before serving.

CHOCOLATE SAUCE

9 ounces good quality semi-sweet chocolate	1 cup milk
	3 tablespoons heavy cream
2 1/2 tablespoons unsalted butter	1/4 cup sugar

1. Melt chocolate with butter in top of double boiler over hot water. Beat until smooth.

2. In a separate saucepan, bring milk and cream to a boil with the sugar, stirring to dissolve. Whisk mixture into melted chocolate. Serve hot or at room temperature.

THE ORCHID

Dinner for 4

Hot Oysters Bonne Femme

Filet of Flounder with Sauce Beurre Blanc and Sauce Madeira

Salad Orchid with Blended Tofu Dressing

Stir Fried Vegetables

Orange Bombe

Wines:

with Oysters: Muscadet Domaine de la Batardiere
with Flounder: North Star, Chardonnay, 1984
or Pouilly Fume, La Doncette

Owners: Richard Wong, and Perry Yeoh

Manager: Henry Wong

Chefs: Richard Wong, and Perry Yeoh

THE ORCHID

Many cooking aficionados would agree that both France and China have produced the world's most original and inspired cuisines. In December of 1983, Richard Wong and Perry Yeoh, two chefs born and trained in Singapore, achieved an artful blending of these two cultures when they established Baltimore's first French-Oriental restaurant, The Orchid.

Both Richard and Perry received their formal education in an excellent Singapore Hotel. Their rigorous 5-year training included every aspect of French cooking from butcher shop to baking; Perry's training, in particular, emphasized a specialty in Oriental cooking. The two chefs describe their restaurant as "three dimensional": Oriental, French and French/Oriental. This last category is the most unusual and imaginative: an entire portion of the menu marries French techniques with Oriental ingredients creating a "complex and unique" category of food that can only be described as wonderful! Filet of Salmon with Black Mushrooms and Bamboo Shoots; Fluke Flounder with Almonds, Pineapple and Ginger in a Beurre Blanc Sauce; and Sautéed Milk Fed Veal with Port Wine, Cream and Bean Curd are as tasty as they are intriguing.

Richard Wong is the executive chef that oversees the French portion of the menu and he emphasizes that the "presentation is nouvelle but tastes are classical." Moreover, both Richard and Perry "work with the cooks on the line to make sure that everything is perfect." Perry heads up the Oriental menu, which specializes in Cantonese and Szechuan style cooking. This young chef's inventiveness enlivens such dishes as: Spicy Garlic Mussels, Stir Fried Veal with Bean Curd and Black Mushrooms, and White Chicken with Julienne Apple and Pineapple Sauce.

The Orchid is a 90-seat restaurant consisting of several cozy rooms, each mellow and intimate. French provincial wallpaper, lovely vases, candelabra, objets d'art and Oriental silk prints combine to create a mood of serenity and harmony. Fellow diners no longer need to debate the merits of "French versus Chinese" food. You now have the best of both worlds under one culinary roof - The Orchid.

419 North Charles Street
Baltimore, Maryland
(301) 837-0080

HOT OYSTERS BONNE FEMME

BONNE FEMME SAUCE
 (see recipe)
1/2 *cup whipped cream*
1/2 *cup HOLLANDAISE SAUCE*
 (see recipe)
1/4 *chopped parsley*
 12 *oysters on the half shell*

White Wine
MUSHROOM DUXELLES
 (see recipe)
GARNISH:
Lemon twist
Radish rose
Parsley sprigs

1. Add whipped cream, HOLLANDAISE SAUCE and chopped parsley to the BONNE FEMME SAUCE . Set aside.
2. Remove oysters from their half shell and place in a saucepan with a splash of white wine. Set aside.
3. Place a teaspoon of MUSHROOM DUXELLES into each half shell and warm through in a hot oven.
4. Meanwhile, cook the reserved oysters and wine over a medium heat until just cooked, about 2 to 3 minutes.
5. Return oysters to their shells. Cover the tops completely with BONNE FEMME SAUCE.
6. Glaze under a broiler until golden brown, approximately 5 minutes.

Note: Admittedly, this is a difficult recipe utilizing many sauces not commonly made in a home kitchen. If you want to simplify the recipe, then make the Bonne Femme Sauce only, omitting the whipped cream and Hollandaise Sauce. Bonne Femme Sauce is excellent with all types of fish.

BONNE FEMME SAUCE

3/4 cup dry white wine
3-4 tablespoons chopped shallots
3/4 cup fish stock
2-3 tablespoons lemon juice

1/2 cup heavy cream
1 cup FISH VELOUTÉ
  (see recipe)
1 cup sliced large mushrooms

1. Place wine, shallots, fish stock and lemon juice in a saucepan and reduce by half.
2. Whisk in half of the heavy cream and the Fish Velouté.
3. Place mushrooms and remaining cream in a saucepan. Cook over medium heat for one minute.
4. Strain the Bonne Femme Sauce over the mushrooms. Set aside.

FISH VELOUTÉ SAUCE

3 tablespoons butter
3 tablespoons flour

1 1/2 cups fish stock

1. In a saucepan melt the butter and whisk in the flour until smooth. Cook this roux for 2 to 3 minutes or until lightly colored.
2. Add the fish stock, continuing to whisk until the mixture has come to the boil and is very thick.
3. Allow to cool.

HOLLANDAISE SAUCE

1 egg yolk
  Splash of white wine

1/4 pound melted butter
  Salt and white pepper, to taste

1. Whisk together the yolk and white wine over a double boiler or in a saucepan over low heat until thickened.
2. Whisking all the while, gradually add the melted butter until an emulsion has formed.
3. Season to taste with salt and white pepper.

MUSHROOM DUXELLES
(Yields 1 cup)

1/2 pound finely minced mushroom stems	2 tablespoons butter
2 tablespoons minced shallots or scallions	1 tablespoon oil
	Salt and pepper, to taste

1. Twist the mushroom stems into a ball in the corner of a towel to squeeze out as much juice as possible.

2. Sauté the mushrooms and shallots or scallions in butter and oil over medium heat, stirring frequently. Once the mushrooms start to emit their moisture, turn heat up to high and continue to sauté until the pieces begin to separate from each other. Season to taste with salt and pepper.

Note: Duxelles is a wonderful flavoring to have on hand. It is essentially a dry, mushroom flavor used in many kinds of stuffings and sauces. Make certain the final duxelles is as dry as possible. It will keep in the refrigerator for several weeks or may be frozen.

FILET OF FLOUNDER with SAUCE BEURRE BLANC and SAUCE MADEIRA

SAUCE BEURRE BLANC
(see recipe)
SAUCE MADEIRA (see recipe)
4 *fluke flounder filets*
Salt and pepper, to taste
Flour, for dredging
2 *eggs, beaten*

1/4 *cup oil or combination oil*
and butter
6 to 8 *tablespoons sliced almonds*
6 *medium crystallized gingers*
(julienne)
2 *tablespoons butter*
4 to 6 *tablespoons diced pineapple*
(fresh or canned)

1. Prepare both sauces and keep them warm in a double boiler.
2. Preheat frying pan with oil or oil and butter over moderate heat.
3. Lightly salt and pepper each filet. Dredge in flour shaking off the excess. Dip in egg. Fry the filets very quickly in the hot fat until lightly browned on both sides, approximately 30 seconds to one minute per side. Reduce heat to very low and continue to cook for 5 to 7 more minutes depending upon the thickness of the filets. To make certain that all sections of the filets cook evenly turn the thin tail section back onto the body of the fish to create a double thickness at that end.
4. While the fish is cooking, brown the almonds and ginger in butter.
5. Lightly brown the diced pineapple in a separate saucepan. Combine with the almond/ginger mixture.
6. Place flounder filets on individual plates. Top with the almond/ginger/pineapple mixture. Ladle SAUCE BEURRE BLANC over the top. Spoon SAUCE MADEIRA around the sides.

Note: Fluke flounder is, by far, the finest quality sold. If you locate a good, reputable fish merchant he should be able to order this type of flounder for you.

Crystallized ginger is available at specialty stores or Chinese grocery stores.

THE ORCHID

SAUCE BEURRE BLANC

1/2 cup tarragon vinegar	Large pinch of salt
3/4 cup dry white wine	Large pinch of white pepper
2 tablespoons chopped shallots	8 ounces unsalted butter
Juice of 1/2 lemon	3 tablespoons heavy cream

1. Boil the liquids, shallots, salt and pepper until reduced by two-thirds their original volume.

2. Remove saucepan from heat and immediately beat in 2 to 3 chips of butter. As the butter softens and gets creamy, beat in 2 or 3 more chips. Return saucepan to a low heat and, whisking continuously, add successive butter chips into the sauce. The trick is to allow the butter to become very creamy without actually melting. The sauce should be the consistency of a light Hollandaise. Remove from heat as soon as your last piece of butter has been added. Whisk in the heavy cream.

3. Re-season, to taste.

Note: Sauce Beurre Blanc is very delicate and can only be held over water that is barely tepid. If it is kept warm over water that is too hot it will turn oily. The more cream you add to the base, the easier and longer it will hold.

If, after all of your efforts, your Sauce Beurre Blanc does "turn," then you may resurrect it as follows: Place a spoonful of the "turned" sauce into a bowl and gradually beat in the remaining sauce by small spoonfuls.

SAUCE MADEIRA

1/2 cup Madeira wine
  2 cups strong veal or beef stock
1/2 teaspoon chopped shallots

1 teaspoon roux (1 part butter
   and 1 part flour well mixed
   over low heat)

1. In a small saucepan, combine the wine, stock and shallots. Reduce to 2 cups.
2. Add the roux and stir until completely dissolved. Simmer over a low heat for 20 minutes. Strain.

SALAD ORCHID with BLENDED TOFU DRESSING

2 heads Boston lettuce
4 jumbo mushrooms
   TOFU DRESSING (see recipe)

Grated Parmesan
Fresh grated black pepper
HERBAL CROUTONS
   (see recipe)

1. Clean the lettuce and tear into bite-sized pieces.
2. Place lettuce and mushrooms into individual serving bowls or plates. Toss with the Tofu Dressing.
3. Sprinkle with grated Parmesan. Season with fresh grated black pepper.
4. Sprinkle with Herbal Croutons. Add more Parmesan, if desired.

TOFU DRESSING
(Makes enough for 6 to 8 servings)

Juice of 1 1/2 lemons
2 to 3 tablespoons minced garlic
1 to 2 tablespoons spicy mustard
2 egg yolks
1 1/2 to 2 cups soybean oil

1/3 to 1/2 block of fresh tofu
1 to 2 tablespoons Worcestershire sauce
Salt and pepper, to taste

1. Place lemon juice, garlic, mustard and egg yolks in the container of a food processor or the bowl of an electric mixer. Blend until slightly thickened.
2. With motor on, slowly add the oil, a few drops at a time. Once the emulsion "takes" you may add the oil faster. The final result should be a very thick mixture since the blended tofu tends to thin down the dressing.
3. Place the tofu in a blender or food processor and blend until very finely puréed. If the tofu remains slightly chunky add a few drops of water. If it is still grainy then strain it through a food mill.
4. Add the puréed tofu and Worcestershire sauce to the dressing. Season to taste with salt and pepper.

HERBAL CROUTONS

Stale bread, diced
Melted butter
Minced garlic

Chopped parsley
Salt and pepper

Sauté the diced stale bread in melted butter over a low heat until it is brown. Sprinkle with the garlic, parsley, salt and pepper. Store in an air-tight container.

Note: Soybean oil may be found in specialty stores. It is very light and digestible.

STIR FRIED VEGETABLES

1/4 to 1/3 pound vegetables per serving
(may be a combination of
any type you desire:
broccoli, pea pods, mush-
rooms, red bell peppers,
cauliflower, zucchini, etc.)

Soybean or peanut oil
Large pinch of chopped shallots
Splash of water
Large dash of Oyster Sauce
Salt and pepper, to taste

1. Cut the vegetables into serviceable pieces.
2. Put enough oil into a skillet just to coat the bottom. When hot, add the vegetables, along with a pinch of shallots and a splash of water. Cook over high heat, moving the vegetables around frequently. If certain vegetables cook faster than others, make certain you add each vegetable at the appropriate time.
3. Add the Oyster Sauce and salt and pepper. Cook to desired degree of tenderness.

Note: Oyster Sauce is available at Chinese grocery stores.

ORANGE BOMBE

1	*large orange per serving*	*Vanilla ice cream*
6 to 7	*orange wedges, per serving*	*Meringue (1 egg white to*
	Grand Marnier or another	*1 orange) and 4 small hand-*
	orange liqueur	*fuls of sugar*

1. Slice a piece off the top of each orange. Cut around the sides so that the "meat" of the orange may be removed, leaving only the shell.

2. Macerate the remaining orange pieces in Grand Marnier or another orange liqueur for one hour.

3. Meanwhile, fill the oranges with vanilla ice cream. Chill in the freezer.

4. Place the macerated orange pieces on top of the ice cream, piling them up neatly.

5. Make meringue as follows: Place the egg whites in a bowl of an electric mixer. Beat until stiff. Add sugar gradually, continuing to whisk until very stiff. Transfer meringue to a pastry bag fitted with a decorative tip.

6. Pipe the meringue decoratively around the orange pieces making sure they are well-covered. Glaze in a very hot oven for 3 to 4 minutes or until golden. Serve immediately.

Note: A trick for a stiffer meringue is to place the bowl that contains the egg whites into a larger bowl of hot water so that the egg whites become slightly warm before beating them.

Pacifica

P A C I F I C A

Dinner for Six

Raspberry Soup with Sweet Spice

Chevre Cheese Pasta Roulade with Fresh Tomato Dressing

Mesquite Grilled Salmon Filet with Salmon Caviar Butter

*Roasted Red Pepper Cups with Avocado Mousse and
Grilled Marinated Mushrooms*

*Fresh Papaya with Minted Honey Custard
and Crystallized Ginger*

Wines:

*with Soup: Peter Lustau Almacenista Manzanilla,
Pasada de SanLucar, Cask 1-17
with Pasta: Vietti Muscato, 1984
with Salmon: Chateau Graville Lacoste 1985
or 1982 Veuve Cliquot Brut Champagne
with Dessert: Asti Spumante, Cinzano*

Owners: Mark Nichols and John Pletcher

Chef: Christine Mason

Manager: Mark Nichols

PACIFICA

Pacifica Restaurant, announces its intention and style as soon as one observes its pink and gray neon sign. The crisp gray art-deco motif of the restaurant's interior echoes the California-inspired menu and dining style that this restaurant so comfortably reflects. Mark Nichols, owner and manager, is the former sommelier of the Prime Rib Restaurant. Both he and Chris Mason, his chef, share the philosophy that fresh seasonal ingredients simply prepared produce outstanding food.

Ms. Mason is the former chef at the Blue Moon Restaurant and former sauté chef at the Back Porch Cafe, both of Rehoboth Beach, Delaware. Her abiding interest in nouvelle cuisine dates back to the mid 1970's when she was a cook at a Towson health food concern. She describes her food at Pacifica as "quite simple really, with interesting colors, food combinations and strong visual appeal."

Pacifica's menu changes seasonally. It relies upon fresh herbs, mesquite-flavored grills, Maryland seafood and imaginative preparation. Chris decries the recent criticism that American cuisine is trendy and ephemeral. She strongly believes that her style and philosophy of cooking, as well as those of many young chefs today, is here to stay. She uses traditional French cuisine as her source of inspiration and, in fact, regularly reads Escoffier, the famous French chef who authored the first modern cookbook. "How can I lighten this dish and do it 80's style? Cooking with new twists on the old ways, coming up with surprising but compatible combinations - that is what cooking in America is all about today," Chris says proudly.

Her sous chef's Irish grandfather has contributed his recipe for smoked salmon to the restaurant's menu. St. Mary's Bouillabaisse, a favorite among Pacifica's customers, is an old family recipe. Pacifica's trademark is gourmet pizza with zingy toppings such as roasted eggplant, artichoke hearts and goat's cheese. New York strip steaks are served with a peppery plum sauce, grilled Cornish game hens are glazed with homemade peach chutney and green peppercorn pâté is paired with a honey mustard sauce.

While Pacifica is responsive to the need for change, it has not forgotten its roots. This intriguing blend of the traditional with the contemporary create a dynamic, vibrant restaurant.

326 N. Charles Street
Baltimore, Maryland
(301) 727-8264

RASPBERRY SOUP with SWEET SPICE

8 cups fresh raspberries (4 pints)
3/4 cup dry white wine
1 1/4 cups heavy cream
    Sugar, to taste
    SWEET SPICE: (enough for
        10 servings)

2 teaspoons superfine sugar
1 teaspoon cinnamon
1 teaspoon ground ginger
1 teaspoon ground coriander
    GARNISH: sour cream

1. Place the raspberries and white wine in a saucepan. Cover and cook gently just until the fruit breaks up. This will take anywhere from 5-10 minutes, depending upon the ripeness of the berries. Transfer them to a bowl and cool them.
2. Strain the berries and their liquid through a medium-meshed strainer so that some of the pulp is also pushed through.
3. Add the heavy cream. Add sugar, to taste, but remember to keep the soup rather tart at this point since the garnish will be very sweet. Chill the soup until just before serving time.
4. Blend together the sugar and spices for the SWEET SPICE. At service place a dollop of sour cream in the center of the bowl and sprinkle 1/2 teaspoon of SWEET SPICE on it.

Note: If raspberries are unavailable strawberries may be used, although the beautiful magenta color created by the raspberries is unforgettable!

CHEVRE CHEESE PASTA ROULADE
WITH FRESH TOMATO DRESSING

6 lasagna noodles	1/2 cup blended oil
1-2 teaspoons oil	1/2 cup red wine vinegar
12 ounces chevre cheese (goat's cheese)	1 teaspoon minced garlic
1 tablespoon + 1 teaspoon fresh chopped basil	1 rounded tablespoon minced onion
FRESH TOMATO DRESSING:	1 rounded tablespoon coarsely chopped parsley
3 large ripe tomatoes	1/2 teaspoon salt
	1/4 teaspoon black pepper

1. Cook lasagna noodles in boiling water al dente. Rinse with cold water until they are cool. Sprinkle with the oil and reserve.

2. Allow the chevre cheese to stand at room temperature until workable. Blend in the fresh chopped basil.

3. Lay the lasagna noodles (drained) on your work surface. Spread 2-ounce chevre on each noodle, leaving a 1" margin at each end. Starting at a narrow end, roll each noodle up tightly like a cigar. Wrap in plastic wrap and chill for about 30 minutes to slightly firm up the chevre.

4. Meanwhile, immerse the tomatoes in boiling water until skin starts to peel, 1-2 minutes. Remove from water and plunge into ice water to stop the cooking. Peel tomatoes and chop them into approximately 2" chunks.

5. Place tomatoes in a saucepan. Add the oil, vinegar, garlic, onion, parsley, salt and pepper. Bring up to the point of a boil then immediately remove from heat. The tomatoes should retain their color. Refrigerate immediately.

6. To serve: Ladle enough Tomato Dressing on a salad-sized plate to cover the bottom. Slice each Pasta Roulade twice, giving 3 equal pinwheels. Place them on the dressing in the center of the plate. If they start to unroll, place all three open sides toward the middle and the pressure will hold them together.

Note: Chevre cheese is becoming increasingly popular and may be found at any cheese store or specialty food store. Blended oil refers to pre-mixed oils that are a combination of olive oil and salad oils, usually 90% - 10%.
Chef's Note: I am not a lover of salt and do not feel entirely comfortable specifying amounts to use. Alter the salt and pepper in this and all recipes to your particular taste.

MESQUITE GRILLED SALMON FILET
with SALMON CAVIAR BUTTER

Six 8-ounce filets of salmon, skin left on

SALMON CAVIAR BUTTER:

1/2 pound unsalted butter	*Zest of 1/4 lemon*
1 tablespoon minced shallots	*1 teaspoon Worcestershire sauce*
Juice of 1/2 lemon	*1-2 tablespoons salmon caviar*

1. Allow the butter to come to room temperature. Place in the container of a food processor. Add the chopped shallots, juice and zest of the lemon and the worcestershire sauce. Blend until thoroughly mixed.

2. On a piece of plastic wrap, lay 7/8 of the butter in a roll shape approximately 6" long x 1" high. With a spoon or finger dig a trench 1/2 way down the roll, lengthwise. Lay the salmon caviar in the trench. Fill it in with the remaining butter. Roll the butter up in plastic wrap so it is smooth and round. Refrigerate until hard.

3. Meanwhile prepare your grill: Season the grill with a little oil. Get a bed of charcoal very hot then top it with a mesquite log or, alternatively, mesquite chips which have been soaked in water for 30 minutes. When your fire is very hot place the salmon filets, skin side down, onto the grill. Cook for 12-15 minutes, turning every 5 minutes or so.

4. Transfer the salmon filets to individual plates. Slice the butter into 6 equal-sized pieces and place on top of the salmon filets. The salmon caviar should be in the center of each slice. The heat of the salmon will gradually melt the butter.

Chef's Note: I do not like to add any salt at all to the butter. The salmon caviar itself is salty; moreover, I do not think salt contributes very much to the flavor of food other than making it salty!

Salmon caviar is an orange-red, pea-sized caviar, available in specialty stores. It is moderately priced and very perishable. If you really do not want to spend much money, then the red lumpfish caviar may be used as a substitute. The salmon caviar, however, is worth a try if you've never had it - it is wonderful.

You may have to buy more salmon caviar than the mere 1-2 tablespoons called for in this recipe. Simply make more butter and freeze it.

ROASTED RED PEPPER CUPS with AVOCADO MOUSSE and GRILLED MARINATED MUSHROOMS

A day or two before your meal, marinate the mushrooms. You may make the avocado mousse now, too, but the morning of the meal is the best time for the freshest color.

MUSHROOMS:

1 *cup salad oil*
1/4 *cup red wine*
1/4 *cup red wine vinegar*
1/2 *teaspoon minced garlic*
1 *teaspoon chopped basil*

1/2 *teaspoon oregano*
1/2 *teaspoon salt*
    Dash of pepper
6 *large to jumbo mushrooms*

1. Heat the oil, red wine and red wine vinegar just until the boiling point has been reached. Remove from heat.
2. Add remaining ingredients, including the mushrooms. They should be quite large as they shrink while marinating and more so while being grilled.
3. When ready to grill, make certain your fire is very hot. Place the mushrooms on the grill. Once the lines of the grill have become etched onto the mushrooms spin them around so that the next set of grill lines creates a cross-hatching effect. Once this has been accomplished turn them over on their bottoms and continue to cook. They will take about 5 minutes total cooking time depending upon their size.

RED PEPPER CUPS:

Buy 3 quite large sweet red bell peppers. Place them whole, on the grill. Continue to cook until the skin is blackened and blistery. Peel as much of the skin off as you can. Do not worry if some black skin remains - it gives them character.
Carefully cut out the stem then cut in half, lengthwise.

AVOCADO MOUSSE:

3 large avocadoes, peeled and seeded	1 tablespoon minced garlic
1 tablespoon dry white wine	1 teaspoon salt
1 cup sour cream	3 healthy dashes Tabasco

1. In the container of a food processor or blender combine the avocados and white wine. Process until very smooth and creamy. Transfer to a bowl.
2. Blend in remaining ingredients.
3. Warm the avocado mousse in a double boiler.

ASSEMBLY: Fill the red pepper cups with the warm avocado mousse. Place one grilled mushroom on the top. Garnish with fresh basil leaves, if available.

FRESH PAPAYA with MINTED HONEY CUSTARD and CRYSTALLIZED GINGER

CUSTARD:

2 1/2 *cups milk*	2 *teaspoons chopped mint*
1/2 *cup honey*	3 *ripe papaya*
2 *tablespoons cornstarch*	*Crystallized ginger*
4 *egg yolks*	*Sprigs of fresh mint*

1. Make the custard as follows: Heat together the milk and honey in a saucepan until the milk starts to skim (meaning it is very hot). Meanwhile, in another saucepan mix together the cornstarch and the egg yolks. Slowly add half of the heated milk mixture to the egg mixture, whisking well and getting all of the egg off the sides and bottoms of the pan and well-incorporated into the milk. Return pan to heat (medium), add the remaining milk. Whisk well. Stop occasionally to see if the mixture is ready to boil. When the milk just starts to boil throughout the pan, immediately remove it from the heat. Stir in the chopped mint. Cool. Place a sheet of plastic wrap over the top of the custard to prevent a skin from forming.

2. Peel the papayas, slice in half lengthwise, remove seeds.

3. Layer the custard onto the bottom of each plate and place the papaya on it. Ladle a small amount of custard into the middle of the papaya. Garnish with a sprig of fresh mint.

4. Slice the crystallized ginger into thin julienne-like strips. Lay the strips out from the mint as if they were spokes of a wheel.

The coolest spot in the milk is the middle. Once that bubbles it is an indication that it will not get any hotter and that it is ready to remove from the heat. Ripe papaya has a yellowish color mixed in with the red, and it is rather soft to the touch.

The Prime Rib

Dinner for Four

"The Prime Rib dining experience should commence with our famous 'Silver Bullet,' a very dry vodka martini served straight up in a stemmed martini glass." —C. Peter BeLer

Clams Casino

Caesar Salad

Imperial Crab

Greenberg Potato Skins

Key Lime Pie

Wines:

Duck Horn Sauvignon Blanc, 1985 or Matanzas Creek Sauvignon Blanc, 1985.
Thomas Govarty Chardonnay, 1983. Croft Port, 1960.

Owners: C. Peter and C. Nicholas BeLer

Chef: James Miarik

PRIME RIB

Svelte. Sleek. Sophisticated. That is Baltimore's Prime Rib. "My brother Nicholas and I acted out our fantasies," says C. Peter BeLer about their two successful restaurants, one here and the other in nearby Washington, D.C. . The brothers were weaned on fifties-style movies. In 1965 they opened the Baltimore Prime Rib, with decidedly Manhattan ambience reflecting a Hollywood upscale restaurant. It is no accident that the Prime Rib is often referred to as "Baltimore's 21 Club," or that it is noted for its "perfect martinis" served dry and icy-cold in long-stemmed glasses.

Ebony walls, carpeting that resembles leopard skin, and a baby grand piano further the image of fifties glamour. But if the ambience is high Hollywood, the food is down to earth. Slabs of juicy prime beef, giant veal chops, and a rack of lamb considered by some to be the best in town are among the specialties. So are Greenburg potato skins (served here long before they became faddish), Crab Imperial made with jumbo lump meat, hot fudge sundaes, and an exquisite Key Lime pie.

Chef James Minarik, a graduate of the Culinary Institute of America, has developed a reputation amoung food purveyors as a hard man to please. He demands the finest meat the most uniform baking potatoes, and the freshest seafood.

BeLer is particularly proud of his fine California-weighted wine list. All of the tuxedoed waiters receive special training and participate in tastings so that their advice to patrons is enlightened. Personally, BeLer enjoys a glass of vintage port after dinner; Croft, Sandeman, Dow, Cockburn, and Quinta Noval from the great vintage years are available from the restaurant cellar.

The Prime Rib reflects not only the personal taste of the brothers who own it, but their outgoing and hospitable personalities as well. An evening spent wining and dining at the Prime Rib enables patrons to share in this reincarnation of the days when opulence was all.

1101 North Calvert Street
Baltimore, Maryland
(301) 539-1804

CLAMS CASINO

1/4 pound butter
1 small green pepper, chopped
1 small onion, chopped
1/2 cup bread crumbs
1 teaspoon anchovy paste
2 teaspoons beef base

3 cloves garlic, minced
16 cherry stone clams on the half shell
4 slices premium brand bacon, cut into 1" squares

1. Sauté onions, peppers and garlic in butter until tender
2. Add all remaining ingredients except bacon.
3. Spread ingredients over cherry stone clams.
4. Cover each clam with one bacon square.
5. Bake in oven until bacon is cooked.

CAESAR SALAD

2 egg yolks
1 teaspoon Grey Poupon mustard
1 clove crushed garlic
1/4 teaspoon anchovy paste
Dash of Worcestershire sauce
1/2 lemon squeezed
1 tablespoon Romano cheese

Pinch of chopped fresh parsley
1/4 cup olive oil
1 Large head romaine lettuce, washed and torn
1 cup croutons (see index for recipe)

1. Mix egg yolks with mustard.
2. Add all other ingredients except olive oil.
3. Slowly blend the olive oil into all other ingredients.
4. Toss the combined ingredients with the torn lettuce and croutons.

IMPERIAL CRAB

1 *cup of half and half*
2 *teaspoons of chicken base*
1/2 *teaspoon of Old Bay seasoning*
2 *teaspoons Grey Poupon mustard*

4 *teaspoons of roux (1/2 flour to 1/2 butter) to thicken*
2 *pounds of lump crabmeat (backfin will not suffice)*

1. Lightly mix crabmeat with all other ingredients and place in individual shell dishes or ramekins.
2. Bake at 350° for approximately 20 minutes.

GREENBERG POTATO SKINS

8 *large baking potatoes*   *Salt as desired*

1. Wash potatoes in cold water.
2. Wrap in aluminum foil, place on baking tray and bake at 450° for 1 hour.
3. Place in refrigerator to cool for 1 hour.
4. Slice potatoes in half lengthwise.
5. With large soup spoon, remove potato from skin without breaking the skin.
6. Cut skins in half again.
7. Brown in oven at 400° for 5-7 minutes.
8. Salt when done.
9. Serve with sour cream and chives, Roquefort dressing, or Green Goddess dressing.

KEY LIME PIE

9"Pre-baked pie shell
1-1/2 medium or 2 small key limes
3 egg yolks
1-1/3 cups sugar
1/3 cup cornstarch

1/4 (scant) teaspoon salt
1-1/2 cups water
green food coloring (optional)
whipping cream

1. Combine lime juice and egg yolks and whisk. Set aside.
2. Using a non-corrosive saucepan, combine sugar, cornstarch, salt and water.
3. Bring to a boiling point over medium-high heat while stirring constantly.
4. Continue to cook (2-3 minutes) until mixture becomes clear - remove from heat.
5. Add a small amount of the clear cooked mixture to the egg and lime juice - combine thoroughly.
6. Add remaining egg and lime juice, thoroughly combine and cook over medium-high heat (stirring constantly) until it bubbles.
7. Remove from heat and allow to cool before stirring in food color and lime zest.
8. Add to cooled pre-baked pie shell.
9. Allow pie to reach room temperature before chilling.
10. Serve with a large dollop of sweetened whipped cream.

Restaurant 2110

Dinner for Four

French Onion Soup

Endive Salad with Walnut Vinaigrette

Tenderloin of Lamb with Pommery Mustard Sauce and
Raspberry Sauce

Miniature Vegetables with Garlic Butter Thyme Sauce

Fresh Fruit in Vanilla Bean Mint Sauce

Wine:

with Soup: Macon Lugny, Les Charmes,
Pinot Chardonnay, 1985
with Lamb: Chateau de Marbuzet, St. Estephe, 1982
with dessert: Chateau Caillon, 1978 (Grand Vins de Bordeaux)

Owners:
Benjamin Gordon, Sr., Benjamin Gordon, Jr.
Manager: Benjamin Gordon, Jr.
Chef: Benjamin Gordon, Jr.
Maitre d'Hotel: Mario Autenzio

RESTAURANT 2110

Most twenty-three year old men and women are still pondering the vagaries of their futures. For Benjamin Gordon, Jr., however, the future is now, as this young man is the owner, manager and chef of Restaurant 2110, a quaint French restaurant in mid-town Baltimore.

It was Benjamin's goal at age 15, while employed as a dishwasher in a suburban Baltimore restaurant, "to own a small romantic restaurant...food with a French accent." His father, a retired dentist, fulfilled an earlier promise enabling his son to purchase a restaurant, on the condition that Benjamin go to school and learn his trade. Benjamin did just that and graduated from Baltimore's L'Ecole de Cuisine in 1982.

He was hired as a sous chef by Restaurant 2110 at its inception, in May of 1984. In February, 1987, he purchased the restaurant and became its owner.

The decor at Restaurant 2110 gives the impression that you are no longer on North Charles Street in Baltimore. With its sturdy wine rack in front, hanging baskets and copper cookware descending from a beamed ceiling, French provincial wallpaper and gaslight-style wall lamps, you feel transported to somewhere in the French countryside at a small, homey cafe.

While the menu emphasizes French country cooking, it also reflects Benjamin's classical training. There is a decided touch of the "nouvelle" in his approach. Such dishes as Veal and Rabbit Pâté, Loin of Lamb with Mustard Sauce, Monkfish en Croute with Dill Sauce, Veal Normande, and Shark in Caper Sauce reflect this young chef's varied interests and strengths.

Benjamin says proudly, "I have pride and very high standards...everything else will follow." Apparently that credo has worked to our benefit, because Restaurant 2110 has been one of Baltimore's most popular eateries since it opened.

2110 N. Charles Street
Baltimore, Maryland
(301) 727-6692

FRENCH ONION SOUP

4 medium onions, thinly sliced
5 tablespoons butter
4 cups dry red wine
8 cups (2 quarts)
  HOMEMADE BEEF
  STOCK (recipe follows)

Salt and pepper, to taste
8-12 1/2" slices French bread
8-12 thin slices Mozzarella cheese

1. Melt butter in heavy pot and sauté the sliced onions over medium heat until translucent. If they brown slightly, that is okay.
2. Add red wine and reduce by half.
3. Add BEEF STOCK. Bring to a boil and simmer for 15-20 minutes. Season to taste with salt and fresh-cracked black pepper, to taste.
4. Make croutons: Dry out the slices of French bread in a slow oven until lightly brown and toasted.
5. TO SERVE: Ladle soup into individual au gratin dishes. Top with enough croutons to cover soup completely, 2 or 3 per dish depending upon the diameter. Top with slices of Mozzarella to cover. Broil under a very hot broiler until the cheese is very brown. Serve.

Chef's Note: I highly recommend homemade beef stock rather than bouillon cubes. The taste is better and the texture is smoother. Also, when broiling the soup so the cheese will brown, it is essential that the broiler is hot enough, or else the cheese will collapse into the body of the soup rather than remain on top.

This soup is best made one day in advance.

RESTAURANT 2110

BEEF STOCK

5 pounds beef bones, cut up
 into chunks
2 medium carrots, roughly sliced
1 medium onion, roughly sliced

2 celery stalks, roughly sliced
1 pound can tomato paste
2 cups red wine
2 gallons water

1. Spread the beef bones out in a heavy roasting pan. Brown them very well in a hot (400°) oven for about 1 hour. Transfer bones to a large stock pot.
2. Add remaining ingredients, making sure the liquid just covers the beef bones. With the lid of the stock pot askew to allow steam to escape, bring the liquid to a boil then reduce to a simmer. Simmer slowly for 12 hours, skimming the fat that rises to the top occasionally.
3. Strain stock into a pot and reduce by half.

ENDIVE SALAD with WALNUT VINAIGRETTE

1 small head Boston lettuce
4 small stalks Belgian endive
2-3 tomatoes, sliced thinly then
 cut in half

4 walnuts, roughly chopped
WALNUT VINAIGRETTE
 (recipe follows)

1. Slice lettuce into 1" pieces and lay on a round salad plate.
2. Slice the Belgian endive, crosswise, into 1" wide slices. Place on top of the lettuce.
3. Place tomato slices around the outside edge of the lettuce.
4. Nap the vinaigrette over the salad and sprinkle with the walnuts.

Note: For a great flavor, first toast the walnuts before chopping.

WALNUT VINAIGRETTE
(Yields approximately 1 1/4 cups)

1 *egg yolk*	2-3 *tablespoons grated Parmesan*
2 *tablespoons red wine vinegar*	2-3 *ounces water*
2 1/2 *tablespoons Dijon mustard*	*Large pinch fresh chopped parsley*
1/2 *teaspoon chopped fresh garlic*	*Salt and pepper, to taste*
1 *pint walnut oil or 1/2 walnut oil, 1/2 olive oil*	

1. Place egg yolk in a small bowl. Mix in the vinegar and Dijon mustard. Add the chopped garlic.
2. Slowly add the oil, whisking all the while, so that an emulsion forms.
3. Mix in the cheese.
4. Add enough water to thin the dressing to a "coating" consistency.
5. Mix in the chopped parsley. Season to taste with salt and pepper.

Note: A good trick to remember in re-seasoning a vinaigrette is: too vinegary, add more oil; too oily add more salt.

This dressing is enough for 6 servings. Extra can be refrigerated; if too thick when ready to serve merely thin with more water. Actually, this dressing is best made several hours in advance.

Walnut oil is available in specialty gourmet shops. Hazelnut oil and hazelnuts can also be used in this recipe.

TENDERLOIN OF LAMB with POMMERY
MUSTARD SAUCE and RASPBERRY SAUCE

4-6 ounces lamb tenderloins
   Salt and pepper, to taste
2 tablespoons oil
   Fresh raspberries, 1 per
   each slice of lamb

POMMERY MUSTARD
   SAUCE (recipe follows)
RASPBERRY SAUCE
   (recipe follows)
Chopped parsley

1. Quickly sear the lamb in hot oil until brown on all sides, 2-3 minutes, total. Season with salt and pepper, to taste.
2. Slice lamb into 1/2" slices. Place on a round, ovenproof plate, slices overlapping slightly, around the outside edge.
3. Place 1 raspberry on each lamb medallion.
4. Heat the lamb on the plate in a preheated 400° oven until meat reaches desired degree of doneness, approximately 2-3 minutes for rare and 3-4 minutes for medium rare.
5. Spoon mustard sauce onto the center of the plate, letting it run gently under the lamb slices until it coats the plate completely.
6. Spoon a few tablespoons of the raspberry sauce onto the center of the mustard sauce, so that there is a circle of bright red in the middle of the plate.
7. Sprinkle with chopped parsley and serve.

Note: Lamb tenderloin is not a cut of meat easily found in grocery stores. Your best bet is to order it in advance at a specialty meat store.
A good trick to make sure the lamb is ultimately cooked to the proper degree of doneness is to cook it in the pan (step 1.) one stage less then you eventually want it. You may brown the lamb 1/2 hour ahead of time.

POMMERY MUSTARD SAUCE

4   tablespoons brandy
2   cups heavy cream
2-3 tablespoons Pommery
    mustard (grainy)

2   tablespoons tomato paste
6   peppercorns
   Beef stock
   Salt and pepper, to taste

1. Make sure your saucepan is very hot. Remove pan from the heat, add the brandy and flame until reduced to about 1 tablespoon.
2. Add the cream, mustard, tomato paste and peppercorns. Cook at a medium simmer for 10 minutes.
3. Adjust to a "coating" consistency with beef stock.
4. Remove the peppercorns. Season to taste with salt and pepper.

RASPBERRY SAUCE

1/2 pint fresh raspberries, chopped
1   pint (2 cups) water

1   cup sugar

1. Boil water in a saucepan.
2. Add raspberries and sugar. Reduce by one-half.
3. Strain through a fine sieve. Sauce should be of a syrupy consistency.

Note: Taste the raspberries first to determine their acidity. Adjust sugar, more or less, to taste.

MINIATURE VEGETABLES with
GARLIC BUTTER THYME SAUCE

1 pound baby vegetables
  (i.e. yellow and green
  squash, carrots, butter
  squash, etc.)
2 ounces (1/2 stick) butter
1 1/2 teaspoons garlic

Large pinch of dried thyme
  or 1 tablespoon fresh
Salt and pepper, to taste
Tomato rose to garnish

1. Blanch each chosen vegetable in boiling water until slightly under-cooked. Make sure that you cook the vegetables separately, as each one will vary in length of cooking time. As each vegetable is cooked, drain it in a colander and refresh it: i.e., run cold water over it to stop its cooking and seal in its color.

2. Melt butter in a wide skillet. Add the garlic and thyme. Return the vegetables to the pan and roll them around in the butter sauce until they are heated through and well coated with the butter. Season with salt and pepper to taste.

Note: Baby vegetables are only available at certain times of the year; if un-available, simply use large vegetables and slice them.

FRESH FRUIT in VANILLA BEAN MINT SAUCE

*Combination of the following
in order to yield 8 cups
packed fruit:
canteloupe, honeydew,
watermelon,
grapes, kiwi, strawberry,
apple, pear*

Orange peel from 1/2 orange
1/2 cup chopped fresh mint
1 whole vanilla bean
*VANILLA SAUCE
    (recipe follows)*

1. Cut fruit into chunks.
2. Place fruit into a saucepan. Bring up to a boil, then immediately turn off the heat. Add the fresh chopped mint and the whole vanilla bean to the fruit and chill in the refrigerator for 4-5 hours.
3. Strain fruit of all its juices.
4. Pour Vanilla Sauce onto the bottom of a shallow bowl (just enough to coat). Lay fruit decoratively on top. Garnish with a sprig of mint.

VANILLA SAUCE

4 cups heavy cream
1 whole vanilla bean

1 cup sugar
5 egg yolks

1. Heat cream in heavy saucepan.
2. Add vanilla and sugar. Simmer for 10 minutes.
3. Beat the egg yolks together in a bowl.
4. Remove the heated cream from the stove and add the egg yolks to it all at once, whisking all the while.
5. Strain through a fine sieve. Chill until thickened.

Note: Unlike some custards where the egg yolks and sugar are beaten together until thick before they are added to the cream, this one uses a slightly different procedure. The result is a custard which is quite pourable and just thick enough to coat a plate.

Dinner for Four

Seafood Sanibel

Louisiana Gumbo

Boneless Breast of Pheasant Stuffed with Game Sausage in Apple Brandy Sauce

Fettucini Carbonara

Belgian Endive and Raddicchio with Scallops Raspberry Vinaigrette

Raspberries Romanoff

Wines:

With Seafood Cocktail: Codonin Blanc De Blanc (A dry Spanish Sparkling Wine)
With Pheasant: Pinot Noir, Robert Mondavi 1983 or Merlot Sterling Vineyards, 1983
With Fettucini: Vouvray, Aimee Boucher, 1984

Owners:
Rudolph Speckamp and Rudolph Paul
Chef: Rudolph Speckamp

RUDYS' 2900

Rudi Paul and Rudy Speckamp, the operating partners of Rudys' 2900 in Baltimore County, have a formidable reputation on the Baltimore restaurant scene, even though they are outside of the city limits.

Paul completed his apprenticeship in his native East Germany before working as a chef in Europe and at the Princess Hotel in Bermuda. For years after Paul came to Baltimore, he served as the "eyes-everywhere" maitre-d' at Peerce's Plantation and at Peerce's Downtown, two well established Baltimore restaurants.

Meanwhile, Speckamp was training in Baden-Baden and Lausanne before launching a luminous cooking career that took him from the fine hotels in Geneva, Munich, Montreux, to Baltimore where he opened Capriccio's and established a fine reputation for Captain Harvey's and Country Fare. The two Germans arrived in Baltimore at about the same time, became professional and personal friends, and eventually opened their own restaurant in 1983.

While Paul oversees the front of the house, Speckamp is master of the kitchen. A dedicated professional, Speckamp is a "chef's chef," a tireless worker who spends long hours at his restaurant, yet finds time to compete as a representative of the United States in the International Culinary Olympics.

The menu at Rudys' 2900 reflects the international background of the owners. Food that is at once simple, elegant, and always fresh features breast of pheasant in apple brandy sauce that has become a "signature item" surprizing Speckamp. "I have no specialties; I simply enjoy cooking," he says, noting that his basic approach is to start with a good product, enhance it without overpowering the natural flavors, and give it a "clean presentation" for the clients.

The wives of both men are also involved and have worked long hours decorating the interior of the restaurant in a style that suggests a European chalet. "We couldn't do it without their understanding," say both Rudi and Rudy, two men who have contributed greatly to Baltimore's reputation as a restaurant city.

2900 Baltimore Boulevard
Finksburg, Maryland
(301) 833-5777

SEAFOOD SANIBEL

2 *small cantaloupe*

4 *ounces lump crabmeat*

4 *ounces shrimp (21-25)*

4 *ounces scallops with roe*

2 *oranges*

DRESSING

4 *tablespoons mayonnaise*

2 *tablespoons chili sauce*

1 *teaspoon horseradish*

1 *teaspoon fresh chopped tarragon*

1 *tablespoon orange juice*

1 *tablespoon pineapple juice*

1 *teaspoon brandy*

Worcestershire sauce to taste

Salt and pepper, to taste

1/2 *cup whipped cream*

1. Peel cantaloupes, cut in half diagonally, remove pulp, and put aside.
2. Remove all shells from lump crabmeat.
3. Cook shrimp and scallops until tender, chill.
4. Peel and cut orange into sections.
5. Mix all dressing ingredients thoroughly until smooth.
6. Fold in whipped cream
7. Toss seafood and orange sections with dressing.
8. Place in chilled melon halves and garnish with tarragon or mint leaves.

LOUISIANA GUMBO

1/2 cup onion, chopped
1/2 cup celery, chopped
1/2 cup leeks, chopped
1/2 cup green peppers, chopped
3-4 tablespoons vegetable oil
  1 teaspoon garlic, chopped
      White pepper, to taste
      Cayenne pepper, to taste
1-2 teaspoons basil
1-2 teaspoons thyme
1-2 teaspoons oregano
  1 teaspoon Tabasco sauce
1 1/2 quarts FISH STOCK
      (See Index for recipe.)
      (Clam juice may be sub-
      stituted.)

  1 tablespoon pork or ham
      base if desired
1/2 cup diced tomatoes
1/2 cup tomato puree
      BEURRE MANIE
      (See Index for recipe.)
1/2 cup cut okra
  2 tablespoons gumbo filé
      (filé powder)
  1 pound crabmeat
  1 pound shrimp
  1 teaspoon cooked rice
      per serving

1. Sauté the onions, celery, leeks, and green peppers in vegetable oil until translucent.

2. Add garlic, peppers, basil, thyme and oregano.

3. Add FISH STOCK and simmer for several minutes until all vegetables are tender.

4. Add Tabasco, pork or ham base if desired.

5. Bind with BEURRE MANIE to thicken to a cream soup consistency.

6. Add okra and continue to simmer for 30 more minutes. Recipe may be prepared ahead up to this point.

7. Just before serving, reheat soup and add the gumbo filé (do not let sauce boil again). Gently stir in the crabmeat and shrimp. Cover, turn off heat and leave covered for 6 to 10 minutes until shrimp is cooked through.

8. At serving time, add a teaspoon of rice for each serving.

Note: Other additions that work well for this recipe are diced pepperoni, bacon, or tasso, a smoked pork similar to bacon.
Filé powder is composed of ground young sassafras leaves often used as a flavoring and thickener in gumbos and stews.

BONELESS BREAST OF PHEASANT STUFFED WITH GAME SAUSAGE IN APPLE BRANDY SAUCE

2 *pheasants*	2-3 *tablespoons butter*
3-4 *ounces fat back, cut into chunks*	1 1/2 *ounces apple brandy*
1 *teaspoon mustard seed*	1/3 *cup pheasant stock (made*
1/4 *teaspoon garlic powder*	*from bones of the pheasant)*
Salt and pepper, to taste	1/3 *cup heavy cream*
1 1/2 *teaspoons marjoram*	*(whipping cream)*
4 *sausage casings*	

1. Separate the legs from the breasts and de-bone all.

2. Put the leg meat into a food processor. Add the fat back (which should be ice-cold), mustard, garlic, salt, pepper and marjoram. Pipe this mixture into sausage casings. Either bake or grill until golden brown and firm to the touch. Keep warm in low oven.

3. Heat butter in a skillet until quite hot; brown the breasts until approximately 1/4 done.

5. Remove the breasts, set them on the back of the stove to stay warm.

6. In the same skillet in which breasts were sautéed, add the pheasant stock and heavy cream, letting this mixture reduce until it is of desired consistency. Adjust the seasoning. Return breasts to sauce and gently simmer for another 1 to 2 minutes or until completely cooked.

7. Place breasts and sauce on a plate. Thinly slice the sausages and fan the slices out on the plate next to the breasts.

Note: Sautéed apples and wild rice work well with this dish.

FETTUCINI CARBONARA

8 slices bacon	1 teaspoon cracked peppercorns
2 eggs	1 tablespoon chopped parsley
2 cups heavy cream	1 pound fettucini cooked
1/2 cup grated Romano or	al dente
Parmesan cheese	

1. Finely dice the bacon and cook until crisp.

2. Mix the eggs, cream, cheese, peppercorns, and parsley in a bowl.

3. Drain cooked pasta and put into the pan with the bacon. Toss them together and then pour the cream sauce over all.

4. Heat it, but not to boiling as that will cook the eggs.

RUDYS' 2900

BELGIAN ENDIVE SALAD WITH RADICCHIO AND SCALLOPS

2 heads Belgian endive
1 head radicchio
16 seedless grapes
20 small scallops, steamed

1/2 cup RASPBERRY VINAIGRETTE (recipe below)

RASPBERRY VINAIGRETTE

1 teaspoon Dijon mustard
Salt
Fresh pepper to taste

1/3 cup raspberry vinegar
1/3 cup vegetable oil

1. Add the vinegar to the mustard and mix well. Add the oil very slowly until it emulsifies. Adjust seasoning to taste.

2. Fan out large leaves of Belgian endive, three large leaves arranged on each plate. Dice remaining endive. Break radicchio into smaller pieces and add diced Belgian endive to it. Toss in raspberry vinaigrette, add the grapes and put on chilled plates. Add the warm scallops just before serving.

RASPBERRIES ROMANOFF

2 1/2 pints ripe raspberries
1 cup vanilla ice cream, softened
2 ounces Port wine

1 ounce Grand Marnier or other orange flavored liqueur
1/2 cup Melba sauce
1 cup heavy cream

1. Place 2 pints of the raspberries in a coupe glass. Chill.

2. Blend remaining 1/2 pint of raspberries until finely puréed. Stir into softened ice cream. Add Port, Grand Marnier and Melba sauce, stirring gently until well blended.

3. Beat cream until lightly whipped. (It should form soft peaks.) Gently fold into ice cream mixture.

4. Pour over raspberries and serve.

Note: Use any good commercial brand of Melba sauce.

Dinner for 6

Mussels in Mustard and Beer

Seafood and Andouille Gumbo

Shrimp Etouffé

Cajun-Style Rice

Sautéed Vegetables

Sweet Potato Pecan Pie

Beverages:

with Mussels: Light Pilsner
with Gumbo: Bass Ale
with Shrimp: Gewürztraminer - Trimbach (Alsace)
or Gewürztraminer - Navarro (California)
or Medium-Bodied California Chardonnay

Owners: Hugh Sisson, Albert Sisson, Ann Sisson

Manager: Hugh Sisson

Chef: Ed Keene

SISSONS

Hugh Sisson "temporarily" forsook his acting aspirations in 1979 to manage a downtown bar that had recently been purchased by his father. Eight years later "Sissons" is thriving and is far more now than just a South Baltimore bar. This "pubby" establishment has always been renowned for its fine selection of beers and wines; its excellent reputation now rests on the wonderful Cajun food added to the menu in 1984.

Hugh Sisson, an engaging, friendly sort, acknowledges the good luck that played such a large part in his restaurant's success. His original chef "anticipated the Cajun explosion by six months." Although the cooking media feel that Cajun food is on the wane, Hugh is confident its popularity will continue. He is proud of his "eclectic customer base" that has remained loyal to Sissons since the Louisiana food was introduced.

Ed Keene is the current chef and his devotion to the principles of Cajun cooking is reflected in the superb food consistently produced by his kitchen. This enthusiastic young man smokes his own sausages and oysters for the heady gumbos served daily. He uses spices judiciously so that the food is not simply "hot spicy" but complex and intriguing. Seafood accounts for 75% of the menu, and the five to six nightly specials give Ed the "opportunity to experiment."

The atmosphere at Sissons is definitely English, modeled after establishments Hugh had visited. Tabletops made of pounded sheet copper are lined against a long wall adorned with beer labels and a world map showing Sissons' diverse selections of beers and ales. The upstairs dining room is more formal for those diners desiring privacy. Sissons even serves steamed crabs on their outside deck in the summer.

For state-of-the-art Cajun cuisine served up with a beer and wine list that is among Baltimore's finest, Sissons is the place. Let us hope that Hugh's acting career remains on hold for a long time to come.

36 E. Cross Street, Federal Hill
Baltimore, Maryland
(301) 539-2093

CAJUN COOKING: 17th Century French Huguenots settled in Nova Scotia (Acadians) and eventually relocated to the bayous of Louisiana. What therefore began as French country cooking metamorphosed into something completely different, since the settlers and descendants had to adapt to local ingredients, such as filé powder from the sassafras tree, an array of wild peppers, bay leaves, etc. The word Cajun is derived from Acadia.

CREOLE COOKING: Usually refers to city cooking, specifically of New Orleans. Since New Orleans has been subject to Spanish, French, Italian and many other ethnic influences, the hired cooks of wealthy familes had to constantly adapt their style of cooking to their new employers. Over time they became proficient in many cuisines and, of course, incorporated their own country-style cooking. Creole cooking, therefore, become a conglomeration of these many influences.

MUSSELS IN MUSTARD AND BEER

6 pounds mussels, rinsed and "de-bearded"	3 cups beer (not too dark)
1 1/2 cups Dijon mustard (hot)	BEURRE MANIE (recipe follows)
1/3 cup grainy mustard	Garnish: extra chopped green onions
3/4 cup chopped green onions	French bread
3/4 cup chopped onions	
2 tablespoons chopped garlic	

1. Rinse mussels in several changes of water until they are no longer gritty. Pull off their "beards."

2. Combine mussels, mustards, onions, garlic and beer in a braiser or deep sauté pan. Steam the mussels over high heat until they open and are plump. This will take approximately 5-10 minutes depending upon the quantity of mussels used. Discard any that fail to open. Transfer mussels (in their shells) to serving bowls.

3. With the cooking liquid still simmering, add the Beurre Manie until sauce has thickened to desired consistency. Pour over mussels. Garnish with extra chopped green onions and serve with French bread.

Note: The "beards" of mussels are loose strands of vegetation that are located between the two shells. As they are unsightly, remove by pulling gently.

BEURRE MANIE

2 tablespoons softened butter   2 tablespoons flour

Blend together the softened butter and flour.

Note: Beurre Manie, or kneaded butter, is a thickener of sauces. Unlike a roux which is the first step in the preparation of a sauce, Beurre Manie is incorporated after the sauce is made. The technique is to whisk in small chunks of the butter/flour mixture to a simmering sauce until the desired consistency is reached. Beurre Manie may be refrigerated. Allow to soften before using.

SEAFOOD AND ANDOUILLE GUMBO

2 cups coarsely chopped onions
1 1/4 cups coarsely chopped
    green peppers
1 1/4 cups coarsely chopped celery
1/2 cup peanut or vegetable oil
3/4 cup flour
1/2 of the prepared SPICE MIX
    (recipe follows)
1/2 pound Andouille
    (or other smoked sausage),
    casing removed and thinly
    sliced
1 quart SEAFOOD STOCK
    (recipe follows)

1 bay leaf
1/2 pound small shrimp (36 count
    or smaller), shelled
1/2 pound crab meat or soup crabs
    (1 per person)
1/2 pound steamed or
    poached mussels
1 pound coarsely
    chopped tomatoes
1 cup chopped green onions
1 pint fresh or smoked
    oysters (selects)

1. Combine the onions, green peppers and celery and set aside for later.

2. Heat oil to 325° in a heavy skillet or Dutch oven. Test its temperature by sprinkling it with a few drops of flour to see if it splatters. Once the oil has reached the proper temperature, add the flour and whisk it quickly until it is smooth and creamy. Continue to whisk for 5-10 minutes to remove the raw flour taste. Do not allow the roux to turn dark.

3. Add the SPICE MIX and sliced Andouille, mixing together thoroughly.

4. Add the reserved onion/green pepper/celery mixture and cook over medium heat for 3-5 minutes, until tender but still crisp.

5. Add the seafood stock, simmering for 20-25 minutes, uncovered.

6. Add the bay leaf, shelled shrimp, crab meat or soup crabs and mussels. Continue to simmer for 12-15 minutes longer.

7. Finally, add the tomatoes, green onions and oysters. Simmer for an additional 3-5 minutes. Serve over CAJUN-STYLE RICE.

SPICE MIX

2 teaspoons fresh cracked black pepper

2 teaspoons fresh cracked white pepper

1/2 teaspoon cayenne or red pepper

2 1/2 teaspoons minced garlic

1/2 teaspoon onion powder

1 teaspoon salt

1/2 teaspoon oregano

1/2 teaspoon thyme

Combine all ingredients.

Note: Andouille is a spicy, smoked sausage found in charcuteries. Hot Italian sausage may be substituted.

SEAFOOD STOCK
(Yield: 7 cups)

2-3 medium onions, coarsely chopped

2 cloves garlic, chopped

2 teaspoons whole black peppercorns

2 bay leaves

2 teaspoons thyme

4 pounds fish bones and shrimp shells (from the small shrimp)

4 quarts water

Combine all ingredients in a stockpot and simmer gently for 2-3 hours. Strain, pressing out the stock from the bones and peelings. Return broth to stockpot and reduce over medium high heat to 7 cups.

Note: This amount of stock yields enough for the GUMBO and the ETOUFFÉ.

SHRIMP ETOUFFÉ

3/4 cup coarsely chopped
   green peppers
1 cup coarsely chopped onion
3/4 cup coarsely chopped celery
3/4 cup peanut or vegetable oil
1 1/2 cups flour
1/2 of the prepared SPICE MIX
   (see recipe)
3 cups SEAFOOD STOCK
   (see recipe)

3/4 cup coarsely chopped
   green onion
2 pounds, peeled and deveined
   medium-large shrimp
1/2 cup flour, for dredging shrimp
3-4 tablespoons oil or butter
1/2 cup coarsely chopped
   green onion
1/3 cup dry white wine

1. Combine the green peppers, celery and onions. Set aside for later.

2. In a heavy skillet or Dutch oven heat the oil to 375°. (A pinch of flour will sizzle when dropped in). Add the flour all at once, stirring or whisking quickly, making sure that the bottom and sides of the pan are scraped. Continue to cook, whisking or stirring frequently until a mahogany-colored roux has formed, approximately 15-20 minutes.

3. Add the SPICE MIX, stirring for 2-3 minutes more.

4. Remove from heat and add the reserved vegetables, stirring well and scraping the corners of the pan. Add 1 cup of the stock, stirring until fully incorporated. Then add remaining stock, stirring well. Return to a low heat and simmer for 20-25 minutes, stirring occasionally.

5. Add the 3/4 cup green onions, simmering 10-15 minutes more. (Up until this point the recipe may be made one or two days ahead of time).

6. Just before serving: Dredge the shrimp in the 1/2 cup of flour and sauté in the butter or oil over high heat until half done. Add the 1/2 cup green onion and continue to sauté for one minute longer. Deglaze with the wine.

7. Add the etouffé to the shrimp, simmering together for 3-5 minutes. Serve with CAJUN-STYLE RICE.

Note: Cajun and Creole cooking depend upon "colored" rouxs as the basis of almost all sauces. The extent to which the roux is cooked, determining its color (tan, light brown, dark brown), plays a crucial part in the ultimate taste of the dish. The darker the roux, the nuttier, more intense the flavor will become. It is important that long-cooked dark rouxs do not scorch or else the dish is ruined! Do not be alarmed if, upon cooking the roux, it assumes a "curdled" look after several minutes - this is normal; the eventual sauce will be smooth and satiny.

All ingredients should be within hands' reach before starting the sauce. The roux is extremely hot and can burn your hands if you are not careful.

CAJUN-STYLE RICE

2 tablespoons butter or margarine	1/2 cup coarsely chopped green onions
1 cup coarsely chopped onions	1/2 cup wild rice (optional)
1 cup coarsely chopped red or green peppers	3 cups long-grain rice
	1 tablespoon turmeric
1 cup coarsely chopped celery	3 1/2 cups chicken stock

1. Gently cook the vegetables in the butter or margarine until tender. Add the wild rice and stir it around in the butter until its outside shell is slightly softened, 2-3 minutes.

2. Add the long-grain rice and the turmeric, stirring well. Heat through.

3. Pour stock over rice - it should be 1/4 - 1/2 inch above the surface of the rice. Do not stir. When stock and rice reach the same level, reduce heat and cover the pan. Simmer for 15-20 minutes or until all stock is absorbed. This dish may be made ahead of time and re-heated when needed.

Note: Wild rice is not really rice at all, but a seed from a marsh reed found in Minnesota. It is very expensive and can be omitted from the recipe if desired.

SAUTÉED VEGETABLES

1 1/2 *pounds, green beans, blanched*
   1 *shallot, finely chopped*

3-4 *tablespoons butter*
    Salt and pepper, to taste

1. Plunge the beans in boiling water and cook for 5-6 minutes or until crisp-tender. Immediately transfer to a colander and run cold water over them to stop their cooking and preserve their color.
2. When ready to serve: Melt the butter and add the shallots, cooking for one minute. Add the beans and heat through. Season with salt and fresh cracked black pepper, to taste.

Note: Any seasonal vegetable may be substituted.

SWEET POTATO PECAN PIE

Dough:

1/2 *stick (2-ounces) unsalted*
    butter, soft
  1 *egg*
  2 *tablespoons milk*

1 *cup flour*
  9-inch pie plate,
    lightly greased

1. Place the soft butter, the egg and the milk in the container of a food processor. Blend together well.
2. Add flour to the butter mixture and pulse the machine on and off several times until a ball of dough has formed.
3. Transfer to a lightly floured surface and knead gingerly until the dough is smooth and not too sticky.
4. With a lightly floured rolling pin, roll out the ball of dough into a circle that is approximately 12 " in diameter.
5. Lightly wind the piece of dough onto your rolling pin and re-roll it into the pie plate. Turn back the excess dough to form a ridge that is about 1" higher than the rim of your pie plate.

SISSONS

Filling:

4 pounds sweet potatoes, cooked
    and peeled
3/4 cup brown sugar
2 tablespoons sugar
1 egg, beaten
1/4 cup heavy cream

2 tablespoons softened butter
1 tablespoon vanilla
    Scant pinch of salt
1/2 teaspoon each cinnamon,
    allspice and nutmeg

1. Blend together all of the filling ingredients in an electric mixer for 3 minutes until smooth and creamy.
2. Fill the prepared pastry shell (3/4 full).

Syrup:

3/4 cup sugar
3/4 cup dark molasses
2 small eggs, beaten
1 1/2 teaspoons melted butter

2 teaspoons vanilla
    Pinch of salt
    Pinch of cinnamon
1 1/2 cups (6-ounces) pecans, whole

1. Mix all ingredients except pecans until well-blended. Add pecans.
2. Pour this syrup over the filling, making certain that all bare spots are covered with nuts. Bake in the preheated 375° oven for 1 1/4- 1 1/2 hours or until the syrup on top is puffy and set. Serve warm.

Note: This pie may be made in advance and re-heated. Serves 8.

SOCIETY HILL
BAR • RESTAURANT HOTEL

Dinner for Four

Shrimp Won Tons with Honey Mustard Sauce

Maryland Crab Soup with Shrimp and Scallops

Grilled Lemon Mustard Chicken

Grilled Polenta

Julienne Vegetables

Macadamia Nut Tart

Wines:

with Won Tons and the Soup: De Loach, 1985 Early Harvest
Russian River Valley (Gewürztraminer)
with Chicken: Sonoma Cutter, 1985 OR Elk Run, Md.
Chardonnay. Liberty Tavern, 1985

Owners: Tom Kleinman,
Judy Campbell, Chase Davis, Jr.

Manager: Kate Hopkins

Chef: Craig Curley

SOCIETY HILL HOTEL:

Blend New York chic with a Maryland/American menu, a chef who has spent most of his professional life cooking on the West Coast and an English-style "Bed and Breakfast," and you have just described Society Hill Hotel. The word "hotel" is actually a misnomer. Kate Hopkins, manager, describes the gracious 15-room inn as "somewhere between a country and European inn, but with the amenities one expects in a large hotel...we call ourselves an urban inn."

Society Hill Hotel's ninety-seat restaurant consists of the garden room, bar and dining room, each individually and sumptuously appointed. The garden room resembles a private, lush Mediterranean terrace; the bar has the look and feel of an upscale coffee house (where jazz piano and jam sessions do, in fact, ensue); the dining room appears to be an elegant parlor in a Victorian home.

Craig Curley, Society Hill Hotel's chef, is a recently-returned-to-Baltimore native. He has worked extensively on the West Coast, known for its "hip" cooking, and has transported many splendid ideas to Society Hill Hotel. His style of cooking mingles fresh ingredients with intriguing pairings of herbs and spices to create appealing, piquant and unusual tastes.

Many of Craig's recipes are original and the success of these dishes depends upon his ability to capture the proper "taste and balance," at times an elusive endeavor for the finest chef. Fortunately Craig seems to have a sixth sense about what we, the public, like to eat, because Society Hill Hotel has received plaudits since its arrival in 1984.

This eatery's menu, which changes with the seasons, tempts Maryland seafood lovers with old favorites served in new ways: Bar-B-Que Oysters in Lemon Butter Sauce and Grilled Yellowtail (Flounder) with Brie and Almond. Many of Craig's beef and poultry dishes are cooked on a mesquite fueled grill which imparts a subtle, smoky flavor that is unforgettable!

If you are ever in the neighborhood on Thursday at 5:00 p.m., enroll in Society Hill Hotel's weekly wine tasting, often featuring local vineyards along with new "finds." While it may be a cliché, dare I say that "good things come in small packages"? Society Hill Hotel is one of those good things.

58 West Biddle Street
Baltimore, Maryland
(301) 837-3630

SOCIETY HILL HOTEL:

SHRIMP WON TONS

20 *won ton wrappers*
15 *medium size shrimp,*
    par-boiled for one minute
1/4 *cup coarsely chopped scallions*
1 *teaspoon ground ginger or*
    2 teaspoons finely chopped
    fresh ginger
1 *teaspoon chopped garlic*

1 *tablespoon chopped parsley*
2 *tablespoons sesame oil*
4 *egg yolks, to seal won tons*
3 *cups vegetable oil for*
    deep frying
HONEY MUSTARD SAUCE
    (see recipe)

1. Sauté the shrimp, scallions, ginger, garlic and parsley quickly in hot sesame oil, approximately one-two minutes. Transfer to a blender or food processor and blend until coarsely chopped.

2. Assemble as follows: Lay the won ton skins out on your working surface. Lightly whisk the egg yolks. Dip your finger in the egg yolks and brush them on all sides of the won ton skins. Place a tablespoon of the filling in the center of each skin. Fold the skins over the filling, corner to corner, gently pressing around all sides to make certain they are properly sealed. Recipe may be frozen at this point and need not be defrosted before ready for frying.

3. Heat the vegetable oil to 350°-375°. Deep-fry the skins until golden brown on each side, about one minute per side. Drain and serve with HONEY MUSTARD SAUCE.

Note: Sesame oil is found in all Oriental grocery stores as well as many good supermarkets.

HONEY MUSTARD SAUCE

1/2 *cup honey*   1/2 *cup Dijon mustard*

Blend together and keep at room temperature indefinitely.

MARYLAND CRAB SOUP with SHRIMP and SCALLOPS

4 ounces butter
1/2 bunch scallions, chopped
1/2 large onion or 1 small onion, chopped
1 green pepper, chopped
2 celery stalks, chopped
2 large carrots, chopped
4 garlic cloves, sliced
1/2 cup cabbage, chopped
1/2 cup smoked pork or ham, cubed
4 crushed peppercorns
2 bay leaves
3 tablespoons flour
1/4 cup dry sherry

3 quartered well-seasoned steamed crabs
1 cup crushed tomatoes (canned)
2 cups chicken stock (homemade or bouillon cubes)
2 cups beef stock (homemade or bouillon cubes)
1/2 pound backfin crabmeat
1/4 pound scallops
1/4 pound large shrimp
1 small zucchini, chopped
1 small yellow squash, chopped
2 medium ears of corn
1/4 cup chopped parsley

1. In a large pot melt the butter. Sauté the scallions, onions, green pepper, celery, carrots, garlic, cabbage, smoked pork or ham, peppercorns and bay leaf for 15 minutes over a moderate heat.
2. Whisk in the flour and continue to cook for 5 minutes longer.
3. Add the sherry and quartered steamed crabs.
4. Heat together the crushed tomatoes, chicken and beef stocks and add them to the pot. Simmer, covered, for 30-40 minutes longer, skimming the soup of any excess fat.
5. Par-boil the scallops, shrimp, zucchini, squash and ears of corn for one minute. Slice the ears of corn into one-inch pieces.
6. Turn off the heat. Add the crabmeat, scallops, shrimp, zucchini, squash, corn and parsley. Let stand 10 minutes before serving. The residual heat of the soup will cook these last ingredients without danger of overcooking.

Note: If your steamed crabs are sufficiently seasoned, then absolutely no salt or pepper is needed in this recipe!

GRILLED LEMON MUSTARD CHICKEN

2 *large roasting chickens,*
  cut into pieces:
4 *legs*
4 *thighs*

2 *breasts (off the bone-*
  keep them whole)
4 *wings (will not be used*
  in this recipe)
Salt and paprika

MARINADE:

1/4 *cup chopped bacon*
1/4 *cup chopped onions*
  1 *teaspoon chopped garlic*
  1 *teaspoon coarse black pepper*
1/2 *teaspoon salt*
1/4 *cup cider vinegar*
  1 *cup chicken stock*
  4 *tablespoons brown sugar*

Cornstarch and water,
  to thicken
1/2 *cup lemon juice*
1/4 *cup Dijon mustard*
  Grated rind of one lemon
  2 *tablespoons capers*
  2 *tablespoons sour cream*
1/4 *teaspoon mustard seed*
  Chopped parsley for garnish

1. Sprinkle the chicken pieces with salt and paprika. Bake in a preheated 350° oven for 30 to 40 minutes or until just cooked. DO NOT DRY OUT!

2. Prepare the marinade as follows: In a saucepan sauté the bacon, onions and garlic (in the rendered bacon fat). Season with coarse black pepper and salt. When light brown add the cider vinegar, chicken stock and brown sugar, simmering for 10 minutes. Mix together cornstarch and water. Add just enough to the simmering mixture to thicken it lightly. Let cool.

3. Whisk in the lemon juice, mustard, lemon rind, capers, sour cream and mustard seed. Marinate chicken in this mixture for at least four hours, preferably overnight.

4. Grill the chicken pieces over hot charcoal basting them with the reserved marinade. Grill only long enough to heat through.

5. Serve with the GRILLED POLENTA and JULIENNE VEGETABLES on the same platter. If desired, you may re-heat some of the marinade and spoon it over the chicken pieces.

6. Garnish with chopped parsley.

GRILLED POLENTA

One box instant polenta   *Flour*
Butter (optional)   *Oil for deep frying*
Grated Cheddar cheese (optional)

1. Follow the package instructions for cooking polenta. The usual procedure is to whisk it into boiling water and cook until thickened. Most instant polentas take five minutes.

2. Once the polenta has thickened, pour it into a lightly greased oblong bread pan. Chill for one half hour or until quite firm. Invert onto a cutting board; the mixture should come out of the bread pan quite easily. Slice the polenta into twelve 1/4" pieces.

3. Dredge lightly in flour.

4. Heat oil to 350° and deep fry polenta squares for 2-3 minutes per side or until lightly brown and crisp. Recipe may be prepared ahead up to this point.

5. When ready to serve, grill the polenta over hot charcoal just until grill marks appear on either side. Serve three slices of grilled polenta per person.

Note: Once the polenta has cooked, you may toss in a few tablespoons of butter and approximately 1/2 cup of grated Cheddar cheese, if desired. Polenta is coarse cornmeal and comes in boxed form, like rice.

SOCIETY HILL HOTEL:

JULIENNE VEGETABLES

2 large zucchini
2 large yellow squash
1 large red pepper or 2 medium
    red peppers
1-2 teaspoons butter

1-2 teaspoons olive oil
Pinch of finely minced garlic
Splash of white wine
Salt and pepper, to taste

1. Cut the zucchini and yellow squash into 2-inch lengths. Slice a 1/4-inch piece of skin off of each side of all the zucchini and yellow squash. This recipe utilizes the skin only, not the inside (which is too watery for this recipe). Cut the pieces of skin into thin lengths so that the julienne is the approximate size and shape of a wooden matchstick.

2. Slice the pepper in half. Remove all seeds and membrane. Cut into julienne slices similar to the zucchini and squash.

3. Heat the butter and olive oil together in a skillet until very hot. Quickly sauté the vegetables for 1-2 minutes. Season with the minced garlic. Throw in a splash of white wine. Season to taste with salt and pepper. Serve immediately.

Note: This recipe may be served with whatever vegetables are in season.

SOCIETY HILL HOTEL:

MACADAMIA NUT TART
(Serves 6-8)

*9-inch pie shell, unbaked (your
favorite recipe)*

FILLING:

3 eggs
1 cup light corn syrup
1/2 cup sugar
1/4 cup melted butter (2-ounces)

1 teaspoon vanilla extract
1 1/4 cups chopped macadamia nuts
24 whole macadamia nuts

1. Blend together all filling ingredients in the order listed. Pour into pie shell.
2. Bake in the pre-heated 425° oven for 15 minutes. Reduce oven temperature to 350° and continue to bake for 15-20 minutes longer.
3. Serve at room temperature.

Note: Macadamia nuts are wonderful, expensive and sometimes unavailable; pecans may be substituted.

Dinner for 4

Shrimp Consommé with Petite Vegetables

Red, White, and Bluefish

Mixed Seasonal Salad with Balsamic Dressing

Haricots Verts with Pecans

Steamed New Potatoes

Lemon Sorbet with Macadamia Tuiles

Wines:

with Fish: 1985 Pedroncelli, White Zinfandel
with Dessert: 1984 Dry Creek Gewürztraminer
(Late Harvest Style)

Owner: Stevi Martin

Manager: John Brewer

Chef: Nancy Longo

SOMETHING FISHY

There is indeed something fishy going on in the ever-burgeoning Fells Point area. Located in an appealingly restored warehouse, Something Fishy restaurant has retained the beautiful brass railings, tinned ceiling and overhead fans of the original building. The result is an open, airy, wonderfully comfortable restaurant that beckons the diner to relax and enjoy.

Owned by a wholesale seafood company, Something Fishy boasts the freshest, most diverse array of fish found anywhere in Maryland. A full-service fish market, open to the public from Tuesday to Saturday, 8:00 a.m. - 5:00 p.m., adjoins the restaurant; here, lucky afternoon diners can select their choices on the spot and have them prepared to order!

Something Fishy will even fly in specific fish for customers if given sufficient notice. They have served St. Peter Fish from Israel, Dungeness crabs from the West Coast, fresh Dover sole and fresh scallops still in the shell, roe and all!

Those seafood lovers who have discovered Something Fishy are now regular customers. The restaurant's popularity is in no small part due to the talents of its chef, Nancy Longo. This vivacious young woman, a 1983 graduate of Baltimore's Culinary School, has created a menu with Stevi Martin, owner, that is varied and exciting. Ms. Martin describes the food as "elegant and upscale," the atmosphere as "casual and charming."

Ms. Longo changes her menu seasonally and creates new specials every three days. Recent choices included: Fried Pecan-Smoked Crab Cakes on a Bed of Julienne Vegetables; Sautéed Grouper with Ginger/Chive Cream Sauce, and a "Fish-Tasting" of Grilled Swordfish and Tuna with Saffron Lemon Butter. Although preferring to limit deep-fried dishes on the menu, Ms. Longo serves a wonderful tempura or beer batter-coated fish filet sandwich for lunch, the species changing daily from ocean perch to dolphin!

If you have a craving for fish, then Something Fishy, a charming restaurant managed by an accommodating, talented group of people, is a great catch.

606 S. Broadway, Fells Point
Baltimore, Maryland
(301) 732-2233

SHRIMP CONSOMMÉ with PETITE VEGETABLES

1 quart SHRIMP
   CONSOMMÉ
1/4 cup carrots, cut thinly
   in circles
1/4 cup celery, cut thinly
   on a bias

1/4 cup red pepper slices,
   cut thinly
12 jumbo shrimp, steamed,
   peeled and deveined
Garnish with chopped chives

1. Re-heat the consommé to a simmer. Add the vegetables and allow them to heat lightly.
2. Add the pre-steamed shrimp to the stock and gently reheat.
3. Divide among 4 soup bowls. Sprinkle with chives.

   This soup is excellent served with warm, thinly sliced cornbread.

SHRIMP CONSOMMÉ
(Yields 2 quarts of consommé)

1 gallon water
   Shells and tails from 1
      pound of 16/20 count
      shrimp
2 ribs of celery, coarsely chopped
1 large carrot, coarsely chopped

1 medium onion, coarsely
   chopped
1 garlic clove, coarsely chopped
8 ounce can whole, peeled
   plum tomatoes
3/4 teaspoon salt
2 teaspoons white pepper

1. Boil the water and the shrimp shells.
2. Add the chopped vegetables, tomatoes and seasonings to the liquid. Simmer for 1 1/2 hours.
3. Strain through cheesecloth and a fine strainer. If the broth that emerges is still somewhat cloudy, then strain once again.

   The food industry refers to the size of shrimp by the "count" (how many are there in 1 pound) rather than by a size description (i.e., small, medium, large). In this recipe 16/20 count refers to large shrimp.

RED, WHITE and BLUE FISH

1 *pound red snapper filets*
1 *pound flounder filets*
1 *pound bluefish filets*

Flour, for dredging fish
1/2 *cup vegetable oil*

CRANBERRY CREAM SAUCE:

1 *tablespoon unsalted butter*
3 *tablespoons puréed fresh cranberries*
1 *teaspoon chopped shallots*

1 *teaspoon red wine vinegar*
6 *ounces heavy cream*
Salt and white pepper, to taste

LEMON CREAM SAUCE:

1 *tablespoon unsalted butter*
Juice from 1/2 lemon
Splash of white wine

6 *ounces heavy cream*
Salt and pepper, to taste

BLUEBERRY CREAM SAUCE:

1 *tablespoon unsalted butter*
3 *tablespoons puréed fresh blueberries*
1 *teaspoon chopped shallots*

1 *teaspoon red wine vinegar*
6 *ounces heavy cream*
Salt and white pepper, to taste
Red pepper stars

1. Cut the red snapper crosswise into 4 equal portions. Repeat this procedure with the flounder and the bluefish.

2. Dredge the red snapper and bluefish in flour and sauté in the oil over medium heat for about 2 minutes.

3. Dredge the flounder in flour and add to the pan with the red snapper and bluefish, sautéing for 1 minute more. Turn the fish over and continue to sauté for 3 more minutes. (Flounder does not take as long to cook; it therefore only is sautéed for 4 minutes, total).

4. Remove fish from pan and keep warm.

5. CRANBERRY SAUCE: Gently cook the cranberries and shallots in the butter for one minute. Add the red wine vinegar, cream, salt and pepper. Reduce to a light "coating" consistency. Set aside.

6. Follow same procedure for the BLUEBERRY SAUCE.

7. LEMON CREAM SAUCE: Melt the butter, add the lemon juice and splash of white wine, allowing it to evaporate. Add the cream, salt and pepper, and reduce to a light "coating" consistency.

8. Line 4 plates with the red snapper, flounder and bluefish. Pour the cranberry sauce over the red snapper; blueberry sauce over the bluefish; and lemon sauce over the flounder. Garnish with small cut-out red pepper stars over each fish dish.

MIXED SEASONAL SALAD with BALSAMIC DRESSING

2 whole Belgian endive, separated into individual leaves

1 head radicchio, cut into bite-sized pieces

1 bunch mache, washed and dried

1 bunch watercress, washed and dried

16 asparagus spears, steamed

1/2 pint California yellow pear tomatoes

BALSAMIC DRESSING

1. Arrange the greens prettily onto 4 salad plates.

2. Top the greens with the asparagus spears and the yellow pear tomatoes. Chill until serving time.

3. Drizzle the BALSAMIC DRESSING over salad at time of serving.

Crunchy Romano croutons or sweet crackers go well with this salad.

There are some unusual vegetables in this salad, all of which can be purchased at specialty stores or grocery stores with excellent produce departments. Their characteristics are as follows:

RADICCHIO: Resembling a tiny purple cabbage, this lettuce has a slightly bitter flavor. It is great mixed with other greens.

MACHE (or LAMB'S LETTUCE): This is a fall and winter green with a mellow flavor.

CALIFORNIA YELLOW PEAR TOMATOES: Slightly smaller than cherry tomatoes, these may not be so easy to find in which case you may substitute cherry tomatoes. However, this is an easy tomato to grow and seeds are readily available.

BALSAMIC DRESSING

1 *egg*
2 *cups salad oil*
1 *teaspoon chopped garlic*
2 *ounces (1/4 cup) balsamic
    vinegar*

1/2 *teaspoon crushed black
    peppercorns*
1 *teaspoon fresh lemon juice*

Crack the egg into a bowl and slowly whisking add the salad oil so as to emulsify. Add the garlic, vinegar, peppercorns and lemon juice.

NOTE: This vinegar is becoming increasingly popular in this country with good reason. It has a wonderful sweet and sour flavor and can be used on its own as a condiment. It is easily found at any specialty store.

HARICOTS VERTS WITH PECANS

1 *pound haricot verts
    (thin beans)*
1 *tablespoon unsalted butter*
2 *teaspoons finely chopped
    shallots*

2 *ounces (1/4 cup) red
    wine vinegar*
3 *ounces coarsely
    chopped pecans*
1/2 *teaspoon black pepper*

1. Snip ends off of beans and steam them until they are al dente, that is, tender but still crunchy.
2. Heat a sauté pan and add the butter. Add the beans and toss with the butter and shallots for one minute. Add the vinegar, pecans and pepper.

STEAMED NEW POTATOES

20 *small new (red) potatoes, unpeeled*
 2 *tablespoons unsalted butter*

 1 *sprig fresh rosemary*
Salt and pepper, to taste

1. Steam the potatoes until tender. Slice thickly.
2. Melt butter in a sauté pan and sauté the potatoes until they begin to brown slightly. Add the fresh rosemary and salt and pepper, to taste.

LEMON SORBET with MACADAMIA TUILES

 8 *ounces fresh lemon juice*
 2 *cups water*

Superfine sugar, to taste
MACADAMIA TUILES

1. Mix the lemon juice and water. Add sugar to taste, depending upon whether you prefer a tart or sweet flavor. Pour contents into an ice cream machine and follow the particular manufacturer's instructions.
2. Let the finished sorbet continue to sit in the ice cream freezer container just until serving time.
3. Scoop a large dollop of sorbet into each tuile and serve immediately.

MACADAMIA TUILES

2 egg whites
3 1/2 tablespoons unsalted butter
1/3 cup superfine sugar
1/2 teaspoon vanilla extract

1/2 cup sifted all-purpose flour
2 ounces macadamia nuts, chopped

1. Slightly warm the egg whites in a double boiler.

2. Meanwhile, in an electric mixer, whip together the butter, sugar and vanilla. Once mixed, turn the mixer down to low speed and incorporate the egg whites slowly, until thoroughly mixed.

3. Slowly add the sifted flour and macadamia nuts and mix into a light batter.

4. Pre-heat oven to 350°. Spoon out the batter into 6" circles onto a cookie sheet. Bake for 10 minutes or until golden brown. As soon as they are done, remove from the tray using a metal spatula to scoop them up. While still warm, place them onto the back of a soup or custard cup and press down gently so they conform to the shape of the container.

5. They will come to room temperature in a few minutes at which time they will have hardened into the shape of their container. Remove them.

Sometimes one or two of these cookies do not turn out very well so you may want to make extra batter to ensure that you will ultimately have enough. They may be made in advance and placed in an air-tight container so they do not become soggy.

Torremolinos Restaurant

Dinner for Eight

Cabbage and Chorizo Soup

Veal Escorial

Saffron Rice

Tomatoes Provençale

Peaches and Cream Roll Cake

Spanish Kiss

Wines:

with Soup: Cosecha 1983 (Rose), Slightly Chilled
with Veal: Senorio del Bierzo (1975)

Owners: Fernando de Lope
Ramon Alonso

Manager: Ramon Alonso

Chef: Fernando de Lope

Sous Chef: Don Fischer

TORREMOLINOS

In the early 1980's, a quaint and cozy Spanish restaurant opened its doors in downtown Baltimore and soon attracted a small but loyal following of patrons. Unfortunately, this gem of a restaurant, Torremolinos, closed in 1984.

However, there is a surprising and happy twist to this all-too familiar tale of yet another restaurant's demise. Torremolinos has re-opened at 8 East Preston Street and, incredibly, is operating with its original two partners and sous chef!

Ramon Alonso, partner and general manager, is understandably proud of his restaurant's rejuvenation. Both he and chef-partner, Fernando de Lope, are pleased to see the return of their dedicated clientele as well as the arrival of many new customers curious about this Spanish continental eatery that also serves tapas from 2:00 p.m. to 7:00 p.m. daily.

For the uninitiated, tapas are one of Spain's gifts to the world! These intriguing appetizers eaten anywhere from mid-day to early evening, represent small "snacks" before a main meal. Torremolinos' version include: marinated mussels, chorizo (Spanish sausage), Spanish omelettes, fried shrimp, and snails. These tempting morsels may be taken at the bar or at a table.

If asked to characterize a typical executive chef, many of us would describe a commanding and imperious person who is both inaccessible and acerbic. Fernando de Lope, executive chef of Torremolinos, is the polar opposite. Fernando is a smiling, warm and playful man who obviously adores his work. Both he and Don Fischer, sous chef, share an easy, bantering camaraderie in the kitchen. Fernando refers to his ever-simmering stockpot, the depository for bones and trimmings of every ilk, as the "cemetery"!

While the two men talk to me about their vocation, Fernando deftly butchers an entire leg of veal and creates a wonderful veal scallopine dish using fresh herbs grown on the roof; Don, meanwhile, quickly begins a chorizo soup and expertly assembles a gorgeous peaches and cream roll cake.

Torremolinos' large menu offers authentic, earthy Spanish food of the provinces as well as elegant and chic city cuisine. Welcome back!

8 East Preston Street
Baltimore, Maryland
(301) 752-5227

TORREMOLINOS

CABBAGE AND CHORIZO SOUP

1 pound chorizo, sliced thickly

1 tablespoon crushed or
 chopped fresh garlic

4 ounces unsalted butter
 (one stick)

2 small heads cabbage,
 thickly diced

3 quarts (12 cups)
 chicken stock

3 medium potatoes,
 coarsely diced

Garnish with dollop of
 sour cream
 (per serving of soup)

1. Sauté the sausage and the garlic in the butter until garlic just starts to brown.

2. Blanch the diced cabbage in boiling, salted water for 1-2 minutes. Drain and run cold water over the cabbage to refresh (that is, to stop its cooking). Transfer the blanched cabbage to a deep soup pot, adding the sausage/garlic mixture as well as the chicken stock. Simmer, covered, for approximately 1 hour. Make certain that the soup is maintaining a healthy simmer since you want it to reduce in volume by about one-half. It should be thicker in consistency than it was originally.

3. Add the diced potatoes to the soup. Continue to simmer for another 30 minutes.

4. Pour into individual deep soup bowls. Spoon a dollop of sour cream onto each serving of soup.

Note: There is no salt and pepper called for in this recipe. The reason is that the sausage is both spicy and salty and no added seasonings are necessary. Before adding the potatoes, taste the reduced soup. If it is too salty add water. Chorizo is a wonderful Spanish sausage available in most charcuteries or specialty stores. If unable to find, then fresh Kielbasa may be substituted. However the Kielbasa should be cooked whole in the soup and then sliced so it will hold together.

VEAL ESCORIAL

24 medallions of veal, 1-inch thick, pounded to 1/8-inch to 1/4-inch thick
1 onion, chopped
2 garlic cloves, chopped
1/2 cup olive oil
Salt, to taste
Flour, for dredging

3/4 pound mushrooms, sliced
1/2 pound ham, julienne
2 small dill pickles, julienne
Fresh ground black pepper, to taste
6 ounces sherry
2 cups DEMI-GLACE SAUCE (see recipe)

1. Sauté the chopped onions and the garlic in 2 to 3 tablespoons of the olive oil until slightly brown, about 5 to 6 minutes. Remove from pan.

2. Season both sides of the veal medallions with salt. Dredge the veal medallions in flour, shaking off the excess.

3. Sauté the veal in the remaining olive oil for no more than 30 to 45 seconds per side. In order for the veal to become brown in this brief time, make certain the oil is very hot.

4. Sprinkle the mushrooms, ham and pickles on top of the veal. Season to taste with freshly ground black pepper. Pour over the sherry and simmer together for 2 to 3 minutes.

5. Add the Demi-Glace sauce to the pan and simmer for another 2 to 3 minutes. Serve.

Chef's Note: Pickles are my own invention.

DEMI-GLACE SAUCE

1 *recipe BEEF STOCK (see Index)*

Allow the reduced beef stock to reduce by half, again, until the mixture is a deep, rich brown and slightly syrupy in consistency.

Note: Alternatively, you may make a simpler brown sauce by starting with a roux (butter/flour) and adding your beef stock to it, allowing it to simmer for 20 to 30 minutes.Although this alternative is not a classic Demi-Glace, it would certainly be acceptable for home use.
If you do not even want to go to the trouble of making your own beef stock, much less a Demi-Glace sauce, then use Knorr's Swiss Demi-Glace.

SAFFRON RICE

1 *small onion, chopped*	*A few pinches of powdered*
2 *garlic cloves, chopped*	*saffron*
3 *tablespoons olive oil*	3 *cups chicken broth*
1 1/2 *cups long-grain rice*	*Salt and pepper, to taste*
2 *bay leaves*	

1. Gently cook the onion and garlic in the olive oil in a deep saucepan for several minutes.
2. Add the rice and turn it around in the olive oil so that the grains are well-coated.
3. Stir in the bay leaves and the saffron.
4. Pour over the chicken broth. Allow to come up to a boil, stirring the rice mixture once to make certain that no grains are sticking to the bottom of the pan.
5. Reduce to a simmer and cover the pan. Cook for 15 to 20 minutes. Season to taste with salt and pepper.

TOMATOES PROVENÇE

4 *large ripe tomatoes*
   (1/2 per person)
Crushed garlic
Dried breadcrumbs

Paprika
Salt and pepper
Fresh-grated Parmesan cheese
2 *tablespoons butter*

1. Rub the cut tomatoes with crushed garlic.
2. Sprinkle well with the dried breadcrumbs, paprika, salt and pepper.
3. Top with the grated Parmesan cheese. Dot with butter.
4. Bake in a preheated 400° oven for 5 to 10 minutes until the top is golden brown and the tomatoes are just starting to "wrinkle."

PEACHES AND CREAM ROLL CAKE

Sponge Roll:

5 *eggs*
1/2 *cup sugar*
1/2 *cup flour*

Jelly roll pan (sheet pan),
   brushed with melted butter,
   lined with waxed paper,
   brushed again with melted
   butter and dusted with flour
Powdered sugar
Peach Schnapps

Crème Anglaise:

2 *cups milk*
3/4 *cup sugar*
1 *cinnamon stick*
   Peel of one-half orange and
   one-half lemon
   Cornstarch
1 1/4 *cups whipped cream*

3 to 4 *canned peach halves, cut*
   into 1/4-inch dice or fresh
   peaches, peeled, poached in
   sugar syrup and cut into
   1/4-inch dice
Garnish: whipped cream,
   PEACH FLOWERS

TORREMOLINOS

1. Make the SPONGE ROLL as follows: In an electric mixer beat together the eggs and sugar until light, thick and lemon colored. With the mixer on low speed, gradually add the flour. Spread this batter evenly onto the prepared sheet pan. Bake in the preheated 350° oven for 10 to 12 minutes or until the top is golden brown and the cake is springy to the touch. Dust the top of the cake lightly with powdered sugar. Place two overlapping pieces of waxed paper on a table and dust healthily with powdered sugar. Once the cake has cooled, invert the sheet pan over the waxed paper. Gently lift off the sheet pan. Peel off the waxed paper, being careful not to remove any cake.

2. Pour several tablespoons of Peach Schnapps all over the cake and allow it to soak in.

3. Make the CRÈME ANGLAISE as follows: Place the milk, sugar, cinnamon stick, orange and lemon peel into a saucepan. Boil. Add enough cornstarch to thicken the mixture slightly. Let cool (it will thicken even more).

4. Fold the whipped cream into the Crème Anglaise. Mix in the peaches.

5. Spread this mixture evenly over the sponge roll leaving a 1" border.

6. Starting from the long end closest to you, roll up the sponge roll as tightly as possible using the waxed paper to help you roll. Transfer with two large spatulas to a long serving tray.

7. Sprinkle with more Peach Schnapps.

8. Ice with whipped cream, spreading it evenly along the top and sides of the roll. Place extra whipped cream into a pastry bag fitted with a decorative tip and pipe rosettes of cream down the length of the roll. Using extra sliced peaches, form into flowers (each slice is a petal). Serve chilled.

Note: This dessert is best eaten fresh, the day it is made.

SPANISH KISS
(Makes one serving)

Place ice in a shaker. Add equal parts of the following until the shaker is almost filled:

Cuarenta y Tres	*Creme de Menthe*
Creme de Cacao	*Amaretto*

Add slightly less *Southern Comfort*.
Stir everything together in the shaker. Pour mixture into a glass. This is best served straight up with a cinnamon stick in the glass.

THE TRELLIS GARDEN

Dinner For Four

Crab Chesapeake

Rack of Lamb

Fettucini Trellis

Trellis Garden Salad

Ganache Bombe

Wines*:

Chateau Ste. Michelle Chardonnay
Jadot Beaujolais
Domaine Chandon Champagne

Owners: Hyatt Regency Baltimore

Executive Chef: Steve Felenczak

*Hyatt Regency Baltimore uses these as house wines,
available by the bottle or by the glass.

TRELLIS GARDEN

An indoor lagoon shimmers alongside the beautifully set tables of the Hyatt Regency Baltimore's Trellis Garden, creating a "waterfront" setting for one of the city's most inviting dining rooms. Islands of greenery and a tinkling waterfall contribute to an ambience that is at once elegant and earthy. Despite its apparent formality, Trellis Garden is a restaurant where local food lovers and visitors are greeted personally by chef Steve Felenczak.

Chef Felenczak, a Culinary Institute of America graduate, started as a chef at the Hyatt Cherry Hill in New Jersey. A consummate professional, he is as adept at catering banquets for several thousand as he is at master-minding menus for the "back-of-the-house" dinners hosted by the hotel to introduce local gourmets to the restaurant's capabilities. The results of such innovative measures to reach the community have reaped benefits for both sides, and it is not unusual for busy CEOs to work out a menu with Felenczak and then host a dinner in one of the restaurant's intimate corners.

Such personalized service is a signature of the restaurant. A total of 42 people work in the kitchen, turning out picture-perfect pastries as well as beautifully presented hot and cold appetizers, entrées that range from a classic rack of lamb or veal Marsala to skillfully sauced seafood, and salads that resemble edible works of art.

"I follow the sun," is Felenczak's reply to a query about his sources for fresh fish, herbs, and the raspberries that are available year-round at his tables. "Visitors to Baltimore expect good seafood, and I have made sure we are supplied with the best money can buy," says the personable young chef, who believes that consistency is the key to a restaurant's character. Team-work among the staff is another goal he pursues, listening to and acting upon the suggestions of the kitchen staff.

While some of the items on the Trellis Garden menu will be found in other Hyatt hotels, Felenczak is particularly proud of recipes (such as the Crab Florentine and the Ganache Bombe) that are "100% us." "Visitors to our kitchen are welcome, and if they would like a recipe for one of our dishes, we are glad to oblige."

Hyatt Regency, Baltimore
300 Light Street
Baltimore, Maryland
(301) 528-1234

TRELLIS GARDEN

CRAB CHESAPEAKE

12 ounces jumbo lump crabmeat	1 tablespoon chopped shallots
8 ounces spinach (cleaned and washed)	1 ounce butter
	1 ounce sherry
1/2 cup reduced heavy cream	4 ounces BÉARNAISE
1 tablespoon Pernod	SAUCE

1. To one of two sauté pans, add butter and melt over medium-high heat.

2. When butter is melted, add shallots and cook until translucent.

3. Add spinach, pernod, salt and pepper, and cook until spinach is wilted. Set aside.

4. In the other pan cook reduced cream until thickened and add crabmeat, sherry, salt and pepper. Simmer until crabmeat is heated.

5. On four separate plates, divide spinach evenly and top with crabmeat. Cover crabmeat with Béarnaise.

BÉARNAISE SAUCE

1/2 pound butter	2 tablespoons tarragon leaves
6 whole peppercorns	3 egg yolks
2 teaspoons chopped shallots	1/4 teaspoon salt
1 1/2 ounces tarragon vinegar	Cayenne pepper
2 ounces red wine	

1. Melt butter in small saucepan and clarify by removing milk solids that gather at the top.

2. Crush peppercorns with bottom of another saucepan; place crushed peppercorns into another saucepan. Add shallots, vinegar, red wine and tarragon. Reduce by 2/3. Let cool.

3. Place egg yolks in small stainless steel bowl and add reduction. Beat with wire whip. Place bowl in a large sauce pan with boiling water (not a double boiler). Continue to whip egg yolks until they foam and thicken to form a soft peak.

4. When the substance of the egg yolks is like a cooked soft custard, remove bowl from saucepan. Begin to whip in the clarified butter, adding it by degrees with ladle until all is added.

5. Season with salt and cayenne pepper. Reserve in warm place for immediate usage.

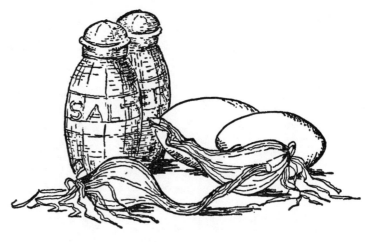

RACK OF LAMB

2 racks of lamb (trimmed and bones reserved)	1 teaspoon each chopped fresh mint, thyme, basil & rosemary
1 tablespoon olive oil	1/2 cup each shitake and trumpet mushrooms
1 tablespoon Dijon mustard	1 tablespoon butter
1/2 cup white bread crumbs	1 tablespoon olive oil

LAMB:

1. Season lamb with salt and pepper.
2. Brush with olive oil and sear in an iron skillet
3. Remove from skillet and brush with mustard
4. Combine crumbs, herbs, and oil. Mix well.
5. Gently pat crumb mixture onto lamb.
6. Place on a roasting pan and roast in oven at 350° about 20 - 25 minutes for medium rare.
7. Remove from oven and let rest 5 minutes.
8. Sauté shitake and trumpet mushrooms in butter.
9. Carve lamb between rib bones. Distribute sauce onto four plates; place lamb on sauce and garnish with mushrooms.

SAUCE:

Reserved lamb bones
1 cup demiglace
2 cups chicken broth
1/2 cup red wine

1/2 cup fresh mint
2 teaspoons mint jelly
1 tablespoon butter
2 tablespoons shallots, chopped

1. Brown bones on stove in saucepan.
2. Add shallots and red wine. Reduce by half.
3. Add demiglace, chicken broth, fresh mint, and jelly. Bring to boil, lower to a simmer and reduce by 2/3.
4. Strain sauce through fine sieve.
5. Stir in whole butter - season to taste.

   Note: Demiglace may be purchased in specialty food shops.

FETTUCINI TRELLIS

18 ounces fresh egg fettucini, cooked
1 1/2 pints heavy cream
9 ounces fresh Parmesan cheese (grated)

1 egg yolk
2 teaspoons fresh chopped dill
2 ounces butter

1. Add butter and cream to saucepan*. Bring to simmer.
2. Whisk in egg yolk; remove from heat.
3. Add cheese, stirring until cheese melts.
4. Toss in pasta and dill and bring to desired temperature.
5. Divide evenly on 4-6 separate plates.

   Use thick bottomed saucepan.

TRELLIS GARDEN SALAD

2 heads Romaine	1/2 cup soy sauce
1 pound cooked baby shrimp (fresh, frozen or canned)	1 teaspoon granulated garlic
2 carrots	1/2 teaspoon ground ginger
1/2 pound mushrooms	1 teaspoon sesame oil
1 cup mayonnaise	1 tablespoon sherry
1 tablespoon brown sugar	1 teaspoon red wine vinegar

Salad: Clean, wash, and tear lettuce into bite-sized pieces. Julienne carrots, slice mushrooms.

Dressing: Combine all remaining ingredients, except mayonnaise. Mix well. Add mayonnaise. Mix well with salt and pepper. Combine vegetables in bowl. Toss with enough dressing to coat lettuce. Portion onto plates. Top with shrimp.

GANACHE BOMBE
12 people

Ganache Filling:

1 pint heavy cream	4 tablespoons almond butter* (*Use peanut butter if not available.)
2 pounds semi-sweet chocolate	
4 ounces sweet butter	

Filling:
1. Bring cream and butter to a boil.
2. Add almond butter and chocolate, remove from heat. Stir until melted and well blended. Cool and refrigerate overnight.

TRELLIS GARDEN

Chocolate Sponge Cake:

3 eggs
3/4 cup sugar
1 cup cake flour - sifted
1/4 teaspoon baking powder

2 tablespoons vanilla
1/2 cup semi-sweet chocolate
- melted
1/2 cup butter - melted

1. Whip eggs and sugar until stiff.
2. Sift together flour and baking powder and fold into egg mixture.
3. Add melted chocolate, vanilla, and butter. Mix well.
4. Pour into lightly buttered or lined 10" round cake pan.
5. Bake for 20 minutes or until center is firm at 375°. Set aside and cool.

Raspberry Filling:

1/2 cup raspberry jam
2 pounds marzipan

Powdered sugar

Chocolate Glaze:

3/4 pound semi-sweet chocolate

1 cup heavy cream

1. Bring cream to boil and add chocolate, stirring until melted.
2. Remove from heat and set aside.

Assembly:
1. Soften Ganache filling and whip with beater at high speed until lighter in color and spreadable, set aside.
2. Cut sponge cake into three layers. Cut top layer in 4" and middle layer in 7" diameters and set aside.
3. Spread raspberry jam on 10" bottom layer, then spread 1/3 of Ganache filling over raspberry jam. Lay 7" layer over Ganache. Coat with 1/2 of remaining Ganache. Lay 4" layer on top and coat with remaining Ganache. Smooth the entire Bombe into a domed shape.

4. Dust a dry surface with powdered sugar and roll marzipan into a 12" circle. Cover the Bombe with marzipan and trim bottom. Place on wire rack and pour chocolate glaze completely over Bombe. Refrigerate until glaze is set.

5. Cut Bombe into 12 portions.

Note: Use serrated knife to cut sponge cake. Marzipan may be purchased in the tube at specialty gourmet shops.

VÏVANDE

Italian Food ▶ American Spirit

Dinner for Six

Carpaccio Margherita

Insalata Vivande

*Red and Green Linguine with Tomato and Crabmeat
or
with Pesto a la Bolognese*

Pizza al QUATTRO FORMAGGI

Sparnocchi E Fagioli

Tiramisu ("Lift Me Up Cake")

Wines:

*Barolo Rollo Zonchera, Orvieto,
Chianti Classico Reserve, Asti Spumanti.*

Owners: Restaurant Associates

Executive Chef: Peter Weiss

VIVANDE

Peter Weiss is, reluctant to talk about his accomplishments, yet more than willing to share the secrets of his trade. These secrets are simple, according to this European-trained chef, who grew up in Switzerland in an apartment that had two restaurants on the ground floor. From the age of 10, Weiss was fascinated with food and spent a year at the Hotel School of Luzerne prior to beginning his career as a chef at hotels.

It was the chef-owner of a restaurant high in the Alps where Weiss once worked who influenced him the most. "Melchsee Frutt taught me the importance of orderliness, punctuality, and the love of one's profession- in my case the restaurant business," says Weiss, who also credits the late internationally known Chef Albert Stockli as one of his mentors.

These days, Weiss is using his full range of talents not only as the head chef at Vivande in Harborplace but also as an executive of Restaurant Associates, Inc. He recently opened Vivande in Baltimore's Harborplace, as well as a second Vivande in Washington, D.C.'s Embassy Suite Hotel.

Bottles of Italian virgin olive oil and balsamic vinegar decorate the table-tops at Vivande, an Italian word that translates into "plate of food." The restaurant's philosophy entails a studied distillation of all that is fresh and natural in native Italian cuisine, with an emphasis on colorful appetizers (both warm and cold), warm and cold toppings for the paper thin slices of beef tenderloin known as carpaccio, pasta with a variety of accompaniments, and imaginatively designed pizzas. Sun dried tomatoes and fresh basil leaves add color. In addition, for those who want a more traditional approach to dining out, entrées such as veal chops and fresh fish grilled with herbs are available according to seasonality, although Weiss expects the California-style concept of "suppering" as opposed to "dining" to catch on with savvy Baltimoreans.

Fresh food, fresh fish, and fresh air are the orders of the day or evening at Vivande, a new-style restaurant with an old-fashioned approach. Vivande volunteered a number of their recipes, enough for a buffet of Italian specialties that will give you a taste of true cucina fresca.

Pratt Street Pavilion, Harborplace
Baltimore, Maryland
(301) 837-1130

VIVANDE

CARPACCIO MARGHERITA
Paper thin slices of beef with fresh mozzarella and tomato.

A dish from the province of Piedmont

1 *pound fillet of beef,*
   cleaned of all fat
16 *ounces of fresh marinated*
   mozzarella
3 *beefsteak tomatoes*
4 *ounces of aged Parmesan cheese*

12 *sprigs of fresh basil leaves*
3 *ounces of virgin olive oil*
   Freshly ground black pepper
   to taste
2 *ounces of balsamic vinegar*

1. In order to slice the meat thinly enough for this dish, place in the freezer for 2-3 hours. Use a meat slicer or a very sharp knife to cut the meat into paper thin strips.

2. Cut the mozzarella, which has been marinating in 1/2 cup balsamic vinegar and 1/4 cup olive oil, and tomatoes into quarter-inch slices. Arrange on platter and cover with beef and slices of Parmesan cheese.

3. Grind pepper over the meat, drizzle with olive oil, and garnish with fresh basil leaves. Serve with balsamic vinegar sprinkled to taste.

INSALATA VIVANDE
Sliced raw artichokes, celery, arugula, endive and mushroom salad

6 *ounces of arugula*

6 *ounces of Belgian endive*

6 *ounces of radicchio*

10 *ounces shitake mushrooms sliced*

2 *fresh artichoke bottoms - steamed, cooled and sliced very thin*

8 *ounces celery - diced*

8 *tablespoons of virgin olive oil*

4 *tablespoons balsamic vinegar*

1 *tablespoon of French-style mustard*

8 *basil leaves for garnish*

6 *ounces aged Parmesan cheese - thinly sliced for garnish*

2 *cloves fresh garlic, minced Salt and ground pepper, to taste*

1. Wash and dry the salad greens.
2. Cut the endive and radicchio into strips.
3. Mix the greens with sliced mushrooms, diced celery and artichokes.
4. In a large bowl, mix garlic, mustard, vinegar, olive oil, salt, and pepper and dress the salad.
5. Garnish with slices of Parmesan cheese and basil leaves.

RED AND GREEN LINGUINE
WITH TOMATO AND CRABMEAT

1/2 *pound tomato linguine*
1/2 *pound spinach linguine*
2 *beefsteak tomatoes*
  (cores removed)
1/2 *pound backfin crabmeat*
1/2 *cup virgin olive oil*
2 *tablespoons fresh*
  garlic, chopped

1/4 *cup finely chopped onion*
2 *cups heavy cream*
1/2 *cup chopped fresh basil*
1/2 *grated fresh Parmesan cheese*
  Fresh oregano to taste
  Fresh ground pepper and
  salt, to taste

1. Boil six quarts water for linguine - add salt to boiling water; cook linguine for 8-10 minutes.
2. Cut tomatoes into small 1/2 inch cubes.
3. While linguine is cooking, heat olive oil in large skillet, stirring in garlic and onions to cook briefly.
4. Add tomatoes, salt, pepper, basil, and oregano and simmer for approximately 5 minutes.
5. Add cream and bring to a boil.
6. Drain the linguine and add to the sauce.
7. Add crabmeat and slowly stir to blend.
8. Sprinkle with Parmesan cheese, toss and serve.
9. Garnish each plate with fresh basil leaves.

PESTO ALLA BOLOGNESE
Basil, garlic, and Parmesan sauce

6 ounces fresh basil leaves, chopped	8 teaspoons pine nuts
1 teaspoon salt	1/2 pint virgin olive oil
1/2 teaspoon freshly ground black pepper	2 ounces cream cheese
2 teaspoons chopped fresh garlic	4 ounces freshly grated Parmesan or Romano cheese

1. Mix basil, salt, pepper, garlic, pine nuts, cream cheese, and olive oil in a high speed blender until ingredients are smooth.

2. The pesto sauce should have the consistency of a purée; add more olive oil if it appears too thick.

3. Place in a bowl and mix with the grated Parmesan or Romano cheese.

4. Toss with red and green linguini, prepared as for previous recipe. (See Step 1.)

Note: Yields one pint

VIVANDE

PIZZA AL QUATTRO FORMAGGI
With 4 Italian Cheeses

DOUGH

1 *cup warm water*
1/2 *cup warm milk*
1 *package of active dry yeast*
1 1/2 *cups of all-purpose flour*

1/4 *cup virgin olive oil*
1/2 *teaspoon salt*
3 *cups semolina flour*

1. Mix water, milk and yeast in mixing bowl - stir the yeast until it is fully dissolved.
2. Slowly add 2 cups semolina flour 1 cup all purpose flour and salt.
3. Mix with a wooden spoon until the dough comes away from the sides of the bowl and forms a soft mass, ready to be blended.
4. Dust the work surface with a bit of the remaining flour - knead in the remaining semolina flour a bit at a time, using a dough scraper and the heel of your hand until the dough no longer feels sticky (8-10 minutes). The dough should be smooth and elastic.
5. Place the dough in a bowl covered with a thin film of olive oil - cover with plastic wrap - store in a warm spot for 30-45 minutes allowing the dough to rise.
6. Press the dough into 4 inch circles with your fingertips then stretch the circles out into 9"-12" pizza shells.
7. Fit the shells into prepared pizza pans or pizza peels.
8. Bake for 3-5 minutes in a preheated oven at 500°.
9. Assemble the topping.

VIVANDE

TOPPING

4 cups fresh stewed tomatoes

12 ounces mozzarella cheese

4 ounces fontina cheese

4 ounces gorgonzola cheese

4 ounces Parmesan cheese

8 fresh basil leaves

8 sun-dried tomatoes

1. Spread tomatoes over the prepared dough shells.

2. Mix the fontina, gorgonzola, and Parmesan cheese and spread this mixture over the tomatoes.

3. Cover with the shredded mozzarella cheese.

4. Drizzle the olive oil over the pie and bake for 5-7 minutes in a preheated oven at 500° until golden brown.

5. Garnish with sun-dried tomatoes and fresh basil leaves.

SPARNOCCHI E FAGIOLI
Shrimp and bean salad in a special Venetian sauce

1 1/2 pounds of shrimp (21-25
      pieces per pound)
  10 ounces cannelli beans
      (dried white beans)
   3 large tomatoes peeled, seeded
      and cut into small pieces
  10 basil leaves - chopped
1/2 ounce Italian parsley - chopped

1/2 cup raw celery - chopped
1/2 cup olive oil
1/4 cup fresh lemon juice
  1 teaspoon mustard
    Salt and fresh ground
    black pepper, to taste

1. Soak the beans in 2 gallons of water for 6 hours. Cook and drain.
2. Peel and clean the shrimp - cook in salted water for 7 minutes.
3. In a bowl, mix lemon juice, mustard, and olive oil.
4. Add the beans, celery, basil, parsley, and shrimp.
5. Add salt and pepper to taste.
6. Mix carefully and serve with chopped basil leaves as garnish.

TIRAMISU
"Lift Me Up Cake"

6 ounces bittersweet chocolate
   chopped coarsely
18 ladyfingers
1 tablespoon vanilla sugar
1 cup espresso coffee, chilled
3 egg yolks

4 tablespoons granulated sugar
2 tablespoons Kahlúa
12 ounces of Mascarpone cheese
1 teaspoon unsweetened
   cocoa powder

1. Mix egg yolks, sugar, and vanilla sugar in a bowl to a creamy consistency.

2. Add the Mascarpone cheese and stir gently.

3. Mix the Kahlúa and espresso in a separate bowl and soak the ladyfingers in the mixture for a couple of seconds.

4. Beginning with the ladyfingers, arrange in six individual dishes alternating layers of ladyfingers, chocolate, and Mascarpone, ending with Mascarpone.

5. Dust with cocoa powder, cover with aluminum foil and refrigerate at least 1 hour before serving.

Note: To make the vanilla sugar, place a vanilla bean in a covered container with two cups sugar.

RESUME OF AUTHORS:

Mary Lou Baker is a free-lance food and travel writer whose articles have appeared in numerous publications. The former food and wine editor for BALTIMORE MAGAZINE, she is an occasional contributor to the BALTIMORE SUN MAGAZINE. Since 1976, she has written a weekly food column for the CAPITAL GAZETTE newspapers in Annapolis. She enjoys cooking for friends, picnics at Oregon Ridge while listening to the Baltimore Symphony orchestra, tennis, and Gary Larson cartoons.

Bonnie Rapoport Marshall is the former owner of Culinary Arts, a Mt. Washington-based cooking school. She has authored two books (DINING IN BALTIMORE, Volume 1 and BONNIE RAPOPORT'S RESTAURANT BOOK), written numerous cooking columns for local newspapers as well as the WASHINGTON POST, appeared weekly on Channel 13's "Evening Magazine" as restaurant reporter for two years and currently works as a party consultant for Gourmet Caterers. She enjoys cooking for her husband; playing with her 24-month old son, Jake; Center Stage; and Rehoboth Beach.

RECIPIE INDEX

ENTREES

SALADS

RECIPIE INDEX

SALAD DRESSINGS

SAUCES

SEASONINGS

SOUPS

RECIPE INDEX

DINING IN-WITH THE GREAT CHEFS
A collection of Gourmet Recipes from the finest chefs in the Country

❑ *Dining In-Atlanta* $8.95
❑ *Dining In-Baltimore, Vol. II* 8.95
❑ *Dining In-Boston* 8.95
❑ *Dining In-Chicago, Vol. II* 8.95
❑ *Dining In-Cleveland* 8.95
❑ *Dining In-Dallas* 8.95
❑ *Dining In-Denver* 8.95
❑ *Dining In-Hampton Roads* 8.95
❑ *Dining In-Hawaii* 8.95
❑ *Dining In-Houston, Vol. II* 8.95
❑ *Dining In-Kansas City* 8.95
❑ *Dining In-Los Angeles* 8.95
❑ *Dining In-Manhattan* 8.95
❑ *Dining In-Miami* 8.95
❑ *Dining In-Milwaukee* 8.95
❑ *Dining In-Minneapolis/St. Paul, Vol. II* 8.95
❑ *Dining In-Monterey Peninsula* 7.95
❑ *Dining In-Napa Valley* 8.95

❑ *Dining In-New Orleans* $8.95
❑ *Dining In-Philadelphia, Vol. II* 8.95
❑ *Dining In-Phoenix* 8.95
❑ *Dining In-Pittsburgh* 7.95
❑ *Dining In-Portland* 7.95
❑ *Dining In-St. Louis* 7.95
❑ *Dining In-Salt Lake City* 8.95
❑ *Dining In-San Francisco, Vol. II* 8.95
❑ *Dining In-Seattle* 8.95
❑ *Dining In-Sun Valley* 8.95
❑ *Dining In-Toronto* 7.95
❑ *Dining In-Vancouver, B.C.* 8.95
❑ *Dining In-Washington, D.C.* 8.95
❑ *Dining In-Italian* 8.95
❑ *Dining In-The Great Embassies*
    (hardbound) 16.95

THE EPICURES
Menu Guides to the Better Restaurants in Each City

❑ *Baltimore Epicure* $7.95
❑ *Boston Epicure* 7.95
❑ *Chicago Epicure* 7.95
❑ *Dallas Epicure* 7.95
❑ *Denver Epicure* 7.95
❑ *Detroit Epicure* 7.95
❑ *Honolulu Epicure* 7.95
❑ *Houston Epicure* 7.95
❑ *Kansas City Epicure* 7.95
❑ *Los Angeles Epicure* 7.95

❑ *Manhattan Epicure* $7.95
❑ *Miami Epicure* 7.95
❑ *Minneapolis Epicure* 7.95
❑ *New Orleans Epicure* 7.95
❑ *San Diego Epicure* 7.95
❑ *San Francisco Epicure* 7.95
❑ *Seattle Epicure* 7.95
❑ *St. Louis Epicure* 7.95
❑ *Washington, D.C. Epicure*

TO ORDER, SEND PRICE PLUS $1.00 POSTAGE AND HANDLING PER BOOK

❑ Check (✔) here if you would like to have a different Dining In-Cookbook sent to you once a month. Payable by MasterCard or VISA. Returnable if not satisfied.

BILL TO:

Name_____

Address_____

City_____ State____ Zip _____

SEND COMPLETED FORM TO:

PEANUT BUTTER PUBLISHING

702 Randolph Avenue

Costa Mesa, CA 92626

BA1187

SHIP TO:

Name_____

Address_____

City_____ State____ Zip _____

❑ Payment Enclosed   ❑ Charge

VISA #_____ Exp. _____

MasterCard #_____ Exp. _____

Signature_____